WITHDRAWN

THE WINTER EXPLOITATION SYSTEMS OF BAY-BREASTED AND CHESTNUT-SIDED WARBLERS IN PANAMA

The Winter Exploitation Systems of Bay-breasted and Chestnut-sided Warblers in Panama

by Russell Greenberg

UNIVERSITY OF CALIFORNIA PRESS
Berkeley · Los Angeles · London

UNIVERSITY OF CALIFORNIA PUBLICATIONS IN ZOOLOGY

Editorial Board: Cadet H. Hand, Jr., George L. Hunt, Jr.,
Peter B. Moyle, James L. Patton

Volume 116

Issue Date: March 1984

UNIVERSITY OF CALIFORNIA PRESS
BERKELEY AND LOS ANGELES, CALIFORNIA

UNIVERSITY OF CALIFORNIA PRESS, LTD.
LONDON, ENGLAND

ISBN: 0-520-09670-3
LIBRARY OF CONGRESS CATALOG NUMBER: 82-17412

© 1984 BY THE REGENTS OF THE UNIVERSITY OF CALIFORNIA

Library of Congress Cataloging in Publication Data

Greenberg, Russell.
 The winter exploitation systems of bay-breasted and chestnut-sided warblers in Panama.

 (University of California publications in zoology; v. 116)
 Bibliography: p.
 1. Bay-breasted warbler—Wintering. 2. Bay-breasted warbler—Food. 3. Chestnut-sided warbler—Wintering. 4. Chestnut-sided warbler—Food. 5. Birds—Panama—Wintering. 6. Birds—Panama—Food. I. Title. II. Series.
 QL696.P2618G73   1983   598.8'72   82-17412
 ISBN 0-520-09670-3

Contents

List of Figures, vii
List of Tables, viii
Acknowledgments, x

INTRODUCTION	1
WHAT IS A WINTER EXPLOITATION SYSTEM?	3
ESSENTIAL ASPECTS OF WINTER EXPLOITATION SYSTEMS CONSIDERED IN THIS STUDY	5

    Population Movements, 5
    Social Behavior, 5
    Foraging Behavior, 5

THE WARBLER SPECIES   6
    Breeding Distributions, 6
    Winter Distributions, 8
    Morphology, 8

STUDY SITES   10
    Winter Season Study Sites, 10
    Forest Phenology on Barro Colorado Island, 13
    Breeding Season Study Sites, 14

METHODS   16
    Population Density, 16
    Group Size, 17
    Spacing System, 17
    Mixed Species Flocking, 18
    Foraging Microhabitat, 18
    Foraging Movement Patterns, 20
    Frugivory, 21
    Breeding Foraging Behavior, 21

ABUNDANCE, HABITAT DISTRIBUTION, AND MOVEMENTS OF WARBLERS   22
    Abundance of Bay-breasted and Chestnut-sided Warblers, 22
    Habitat Distribution of Warblers, 22

Seasonal and Annual Variation in Warbler Abundance, 24
Relative Abundance of Warblers and Resident Foliage-gleaners, 25
Spatial Distribution of Warblers in the BCI Forest, 27

GROUP SIZE IN BAY-BREASTED AND CHESTNUT-SIDED WARBLERS ... 30
Bay-breasted Warbler, 30
Chestnut-sided Warbler, 33

MIXED SPECIES FLOCKING ... 35

CLOSE ASSOCIATES OF WARBLERS ... 43

SUPPLANTATIONS AND CHASES ... 47

SPACING BEHAVIOR ... 49
Bay-breasted Warbler, 49
Chestnut-sided Warbler, 50

THE BEHAVIOR OF WARBLERS AT ANTWREN FLOCKS ... 55

WINTER FORAGING BEHAVIOR ... 56
Foraging Height Distribution, 56
Foraging Substrate, 59
Foliage Arrangements Around Foraging Warblers, 62
Other Foraging Microhabitat Variables, 65
Foraging Behavior, 67
Opportunistic Foraging in Bay-breasted Warblers, 71
Frugivory in Warblers, 71
Overall Foraging Similarities Among Foliage-gleaning Birds on BCI, 76

BREEDING SEASON FORAGING BEHAVIOR ... 79

DISCUSSION ... 85
Possible Foraging Advantages, 86
The Relationship Between Social Behavior and Predation, 88
Mixed Species Flocking, 89
Probable Breeding Season Influence on Winter Exploitation Systems, 90
The Evolution of Winter Exploitation Systems in *Dendroica*, 93
Warblers as an Ecological Unit in the BCI Forest, 95

CONCLUDING REMARKS ... 97

Appendix, 99
Literature Cited, 101

List of Figures

1. Breeding and winter ranges of Bay-breased and Chestnut-sided warblers, 7
2. Monthly rainfall on BCI during study, 11
3. Long-term average monthly rainfall for BCI and Darien, 12
4. Number of arthropods on foliage censuses, 15
5. Dispersion of Bay-breased Warblers along the Wheeler transect, 27
6. Dispersion of Bay-breasted Warblers along the Snyder-Molino transect, 28
7. Scatter plot of Bay-breasted Warbler and resident insectivore sightings along BCI transects, 29
8. "Alliances" of species that tend to co-occurr in mixed species flocks, 41
9. Scatter diagram of Close Association index values and foraging height overlaps for flocking species and Bay-breasted and Chestnut-sided warblers, 45
10. Temporal pattern of resightings of marked or recognizable Bay-breasted Warblers, 50
11. The distribution of sightings of some Chestnut-sided Warblers on the BCI plateau, 52
12. Sightings of Chestnut-sided Warblers along major trail systems on BCI, 53
13. Sound spectographs of two territorial calls of Chestnut-sided Warblers, 54
14. Foraging height distributions of Bay-breasted and Chestnut-sided warblers in different seasons, 57
15. Scatter diagram of foraging height versus tree height in Bay-breasted and Chestnut-sided warblers, 57
16. Foraging height distribution and branch density in different forest types on BCI, 58
17. Foraging height distributions for foliage-gleaning birds, 60
18. Frugivory index values per month for (a) Bay-breasted and (b) Chestnut-sided warblers, 72
19. Proportion of Bay-breasted Warblers in different molt classes per five-day period (1979), 75
20. Dendogram based on product overlap values between seven species of foliage gleaning birds on BCI, 77
21. Percentage of foraging warblers, with foliage within certain distances overhead, 80
22. Percentage of foraging warblers, with foliage within certain distances along the same branch (Maine), 81

List of Tables

1. Measurements of Bay-breasted and Chestnut-sided warblers, 9
2. Foraging variables, 19
3. Densities of Bay-breasted and Chestnut-sided warblers, 23
4. Relative densities of common foliage-gleaning birds, 26
5. Group size of Bay-breasted Warbler, 31
6. Group size of Bay-breasted Warbler in and out of mixed-species flocks, 31
7. Number of Bay-breasted Warblers per mixed-species flock, 32
8. Group size of Chestnut-sided Warbler, 33
9. Number of Chestnut-sided Warblers per mixed-species flock, 34
10. Participation in mixed-species flocks by Bay-breasted and Chestnut-sided warblers, 36
11. Frequency of flocking species in mixed-species flocks with and without *Dendroica*, 37
12. Frequency of flocking species in mixed-species flocks with and without Bay-breasted Warblers, 38
13. Frequency of flocking species in mixed-species flocks with and without Chestnut-sided Warblers, 38
14. Frequency of occurrence of flocking species in flocks with Chestnut-sided or Bay-breasted warblers (not both), 39
15. Significant association between flocking species, 40
16. Common flocking associates of Bay-breasted Warblers in the Pirre Region, 42
17. Close associates of Bay-breasted and Chestnut-sided warblers, 44
18. Chases and supplantations involving warblers, 48
19. Foraging substrates of foliage-gleaning birds on BCI, 61
20. Percentage use of different leaf arrangements by foliage-gleaning birds, 63
21. Availability of different foliage arrangements, 64
22. Chi-square analysis of foliage-use and foliage availability, 64
23. Perch sizes used by foliage-gleaning birds, 66
24. Leaf sizes of plants used by foliage-gleaning birds, 67
25. Percentage of crown cover over foliage-gleaning birds, 68
26. Foraging attack method of foliage-gleaning birds, 69
27. Locomotory patterns of Bay-breasted and Chestnut-sided warblers on BCI, 70

28. Percentage of individuals of various foliage-gleaning species foraging on plant material, 73
29. Nutritional composition of two fruits preferred by warblers, 74
30. Proportional use of foraging substrates of *Dendroica* in Maine, 79
31. Foraging movements of *Dendroica* in Maine, 82
32. Proportion of foraging attack methods for *Dendroica* in Maine, 83
33. Summary of foraging ecology of *Dendroica* in Maine, 84
34. Summary of winter exploitation systems of Bay-breasted and Chestnut-sided warblers on BCI, 85
35. Body weights of active foliage-gleaning birds in a lowland Panamanian forest, 91
36. Leaf surface preference of some Northeastern *Dendroica* warblers, 94
37. Possible evolutionary basis for divergent winter exploitation systems in *Dendroica*, 95

Acknowledgments

I am grateful to F. A. Pitelka for his help and guidance through my undergraduate and graduate years. J. Gradwohl helped tremendously in every aspect of the field work, analysis, and manuscript preparation. I benefited from ideas and criticisms of the eco-lunch and bird groups at UC Berkeley. I particularly thank Bill Glanz, Pete Myers, and Van Remsen for their encouragement. The students and staff of Smithsonian Tropical Research Institute provided an environment of jungle camaraderie on Barro Colorado Island (BCI). I particularly thank N. Brokaw, S. Farabaugh, R. Foster, E. Leigh, K. Milton, N. Smith, and A. Worthington. E. S. Morton introduced me to some of the wonders of Panama, and Bill Glanz and Peter Egan showed me the Maine woods. The following people patiently read through drafts of this paper: F. A. Pitelka, H. G. Baker, H. Greene, and J. Gradwohl. Rose Anne White steered the manuscript through all stages of editing and production. Research was supported by grants from the Chapman fund, a Noble fellowship from the Smithsonian Tropical Research Institute, the Environmental Sciences Program of the Smithsonian Institution, an NSF doctoral dissertation improvement grant, a fellowship from the John Tinker Foundation through the UC Berkeley Center for Latin American Studies, Phi Beta Kappa, UC Berkeley Zoology Department, and the Kellogg Fund of the Museum of Vertebrate Zoology. I acknowledge the support of the Annie Alexander Fellowship during a critical period of data analysis.

INTRODUCTION

Migration provides a challenge to the understanding of adaptation in many animals. Birds, in particular, often move between habitats that are radically different in their structure and food supply. In addition, many birds migrate from relatively simple communities of mid- and high latitudes to more species-rich tropical communities. The role of different seasonal regimes in shaping life history strategies and morphological and behavioral adaptations is only beginning to be understood (Bennett 1980; Fretwell 1972, 1980; Greenberg 1980a, b; Lack 1968; Salomenson 1955). Given the color and charm of many neotropical migrant birds, it is not surprising that many pioneer workers on tropical bird ecology commented upon them extensively (Bond 1957; Chapman 1938; Skutch 1957; Willis 1966). Still, despite the recognized importance of the nonbreeding season in migrant bird ecology (see Keast and Morton et al. 1980), the number of detailed studies of individual migrant species in their tropical homes are few (but see Bennett 1980; Chipley 1980; Nisbett and Medway 1972; Rabenold 1980; Rappole and Warner 1980; Schwartz 1964).

Most of the interest in migrants wintering in the Neotropics has centered on two major questions:

1. What is the ecological role of migrants in tropical areas; or how do migrants interact with residents (Miller 1963; MacArthur 1972; Slud 1960; Tramer 1974; Willis 1966)?
2. What are the modes of ecological segregation among migrant species in the nonbreeding season (Lack and Lack 1972; MacArthur 1958; Terborgh and Faaborg 1980). Related to the latter question, Salomenson (1955) has hypothesized that sympatric congeners tend to winter allopatrically to reduce competition (Chipley 1980; MacArthur 1958).

The problem of the role of migrants in tropical communities was perhaps best introduced by MacArthur (1972) who pointed out that annually the bulk of nearly one billion songbirds funnels into the relatively small land areas of the West Indies, Central America, and northern South America. Miller (1963) touched off a debate when he suggested that the presence of insectivorous migrants may depress the abundance of insects sufficiently to influence the breeding season of resident species in an equatorial cloud forest. Slud (1964) and Willis (1966) proposed that migrants tend to use resources and habitats that, because of their patchy or ephemeral nature, are unusable for stable populations of resident birds. On a biogeographical scale, migrants winter more commonly in areas with less diverse avifaunas such as in northern Central America or the West Indies; on a regional level migrants occur in second growth and high elevation habitats; and on a community level, migrants use temporally less predictable resources. Willis (1966) supported this view with data on the behavior of migrants at army ant swarms, where migrants generally follow the less predictable surface swarming species. The view of Miller, as well as Willis and others, assumes that competition between migrants and residents is important, whether in restricting the breeding of residents or in restricting the distribution of migrants.

A diversity of strategies appears to characterize migrants wintering in tropical areas. While many of the generalizations, such as those proposed by Slud (1964), Willis (1966), Leck (1972), and Karr (1976), may be true, they obscure the interesting variation found among different species of migrants (Hespenheide 1980; Morton 1980; Tramer and Kemp 1980). The most recent work of Willis (1980) on Barro Colorado Island (BCI) recognizes a range of winter strategies. Morton (1980) proposed that migrants have the same range of ecological types as are found among small resident forest birds. These observations suggest that the attempts to define the role of migrants in tropical communities must rely more heavily on good description of the diversity of behavior found among migrant species.

While an increasingly well-resolved picture has been developed for the different ways that birds forage in temperate zone breeding communities (Holmes et al. 1979; MacArthur 1958; Morse 1971; Root 1967; Williamson 1971), the current understanding of the "organization" of assemblages of wintering migrants is far less advanced. MacArthur (1958) suggested that migrants forage in a similar manner during the breeding and nonbreeding seasons; coexistence is facilitated by similar mechanisms of complementary foraging behavior. Parnell (1969) found that migrating parulids foraged in a manner as similar to breeding season foraging as the local habitat allowed. The data of Lack and Lack (1972) for warblers wintering in Jamaica support the importance of fine scale foraging and microhabitat segregation. Chipley (1980), however, emphasized the importance of allopatry as a mechanism to reduce competition between ecologically similar migrants during the winter. Terborgh and Faaborg (1980) suggested that winter species assemblages are governed by ecological assembly rules. Allowable combinations are formed by continual testing as a consequence of constantly expanding winter ranges. By this model, allopatry and foraging differences interact to mold winter assemblages of migrants.

While migrants often dominate their temperate zone breeding communities, particularly among foliage and aerial insectivores, they are often only a small component of more diverse tropical avifaunas during the winter in Central and South America. Discussion of foraging complementarity, geographic displacement, and assembly rules of migrant "communities" calls for the largely untested assumption that migrants form some sort of discrete ecological unit. If migrants have diverse ecological strategies and are more similar to resident species than they are to each other, then the question of what determines migrant community structure becomes moot. Once again, detailed information on the diversity of winter exploitation systems becomes crucial.

WHAT IS A WINTER EXPLOITATION SYSTEM?

On a proximate level, the social system of a population probably influences the kind of food resources that an individual will encounter (Crook 1965). While foraging behavior largely determines the type of prey sought and captured, the overall spacing system of a population determines the nature of the food source that an individual can potentially use. The social behavior sets limits on how a population can respond to fluctuating or patchy food supplies. Orians (1961), for example, showed that two similar, syntopically breeding species of *Agelaius* blackbirds use radically different food sources, related to their different social systems.

The concept that foraging and social behavior interact to determine resource use was formalized in the term exploitation system defined by Pitelka et al. (1974) to be "that pattern of deployment and activities of members of a population in space and time adaptively serving the needs of self maintenance and successful reproduction in relation to a given environment." Their review of breeding dispersion of calidridine sandpipers suggested that the exploitation systems allowed individuals of opportunistic social systems (polygamy, promiscuity, semi-coloniality, etc.) and annually fluctuating populations to use more variable resources and individuals of species with conservative social systems (monogamy) to depend on a more constant resource base.

The exploitation system concept can be easily applied to passerines wintering in tropical habitats. On a proximate level, the deployments and activities of individuals can greatly alter the nature of the resources used by individuals; opportunistic and conservative strategies are easily conceived. Because of large scale movements or within-community wandering, individuals employing an opportunistic strategy could have little commitment to the resources in a local area; rather, they might concentrate on locally or temporally abundant food. Conservative species could give up access to rich but temporary food supplies to invest, through territorial defense, in a patch that is productive throughout the winter.

Migrants on their wintering range seem to show significant variation in foraging and social behavior. Further, the scanty data indicate a relationship between the two aspects of winter exploitation systems. Eaton (1953) noted such a relationship among warblers wintering in Cuba. Forest insectivores were solitary and probably territorial, whereas the open-country Palm Warbler (*Dendroica palmarum*) formed single species flocks. Skutch (1957) described an incredible diversity of winter social behavior among warblers wintering in Central America. Morton (1980) placed the social behavior of migrants in the context of adaptation to seasonal change within tropical areas. He proposed that territorial species are restricted to the most mesic and seasonally stable habitats. Within the genus *Dendroica* (Greenberg 1979), species with the most labile foraging behavior are those that tend to be the most intraspecifically gregarious. Despite these observations, the degree of variation in social organization and foraging behavior among wintering migrants, as well as the interrelationship of these components of winter exploitation systems, has yet to be studied in any quantitative sense. It is this gap that the following study begins to fill.

ESSENTIAL ASPECTS OF WINTER EXPLOITATION SYSTEMS CONSIDERED IN THIS STUDY

POPULATION MOVEMENTS

Movement may consist of slow drift through a region, which apparently occurs in several species of South American wintering migrants moving though the Isthmus of Panama (Willis 1966; Hespenheide 1980; Morton 1980), or it may consist of nomadic wandering. From the viewpoint of a single community, such movements manifest themselves as dramatic fluctuations in local population size.

SOCIAL BEHAVIOR

Spacing systems. I recognize two critical components of warbler spacing behavior: site tenacity, i.e., the degree to which individuals remain localized throughout a winter; and the exclusiveness of home range use, i.e., the amount that the daily range of one individual overlaps the ranges of other individuals. On one extreme, species that occupy small non-overlapping home ranges are territorial. Territoriality is defined, in this study, primarily on the basis of exclusiveness or dominance of individuals in an area (Pitelka 1959; Willis 1967). The observation of boundary-oriented displays is considered strong corroborative evidence, but in dense tropical forest vegetation subtle displays are often missed.

Intraspecific Gregariousness. The tendency of individuals to occur in close proximity to conspecifics without overt aggression. This includes integrated single species flocks as well as aggregations at fruiting trees.

Mixed Species Flocking. The degree to which mixed species flocks are joined and the species with which a warbler species tends to co-occur.

Dominance Interactions. Supplantations, chases, or displays that might indicate dominance interactions between individuals of a warbler species, or between warblers and other species.

FORAGING BEHAVIOR

Insectivorous Foraging Behavior and Microhabitat. The foraging strata, substrates, search, and attack behavior that characterize a warbler species.

Variation in Modal Foraging Behavior. The variation within and between seasons in the major features of insectivorous foraging behavior.

Degree of Omnivory. The degree and seasonality of nectarivory and frugivory.

THE WARBLER SPECIES

Two species of arboreal wood warblers, Bay-breasted (*Dendroica castanea*) and Chestnut-sided warblers (*Dendroica pensylvanica*) winter commonly in the forests and woodlands of Panama (Eisenmann 1957; Morton 1980). Beside being closely related and morphologically similar, these two species are at least superficially similar in ecology (Willis 1966, 1980). During the winters from December 1976 through May 1980, I examined aspects of their winter exploitation systems. I assessed the similarity of the overall winter exploitation systems to those of resident foliage gleaning birds to determine if these congeneric migrants form any sort of ecological unit in their winter community. In addition, I studied both species in Central Maine June-July 1980 to establish the relationship between breeding and wintering foraging ecology.

BREEDING DISTRIBUTIONS

Bay-breasted and Chestnut-sided warblers are largely allopatric on the breeding range (Fig. 1). Where they do overlap, the two species have distinct habitat preferences and true syntopy is rare. The Bay-breasted Warbler is restricted to the southeasterly portion of the boreal forests, exclusive of most of the Appalachian Mountains. It rarely occurs northwest of Ontario as a breeding species (Sealy 1979). Within this region of the boreal forest the Bay-breasted Warbler is regularly syntopic with several congeners (Kendeigh 1947; MacArthur 1958): Black-throated Green (*Dendroica virens*); Blackburnian (*D. fusca*); Cape May (*D. tigrina*); Magnolia (*D. magnolia*); and Myrtle warblers (*D. coronata*). The Bay-breasted Warbler prefers more forested habitat than the bog-loving Palm Warbler (Erskine 1977) and is separated largely by habitat from the morphologically similar Blackpoll Warbler (*Dendroica striata*) (Morse 1979). The Bay-breasted Warbler is particularly common in areas of spruce budworm gradations (Kendeigh 1947; Mook 1963; Morris et al. 1958; Morse 1978).

The Chestnut-sided Warbler is the common *Dendroica* of successional broad-leafed habitats in northeastern North America. Because of its similar habitat preference, it commonly co-occurs with Yellow Warbler (*Dendroica petechia*). Presently The Chestnut-sided Warbler is widespread and abundant, but before the clearing of mature deciduous forests in the early nineteenth century Chestnut-sided Warblers were quite scarce (Bent 1953). Like the Prairie Warbler (*D. discolor* (Nolan 1979), the Chestnut-sided Warbler has increased to occupy the abundant second-growth habitats resulting from continual clearing of the forests and later abandonment.

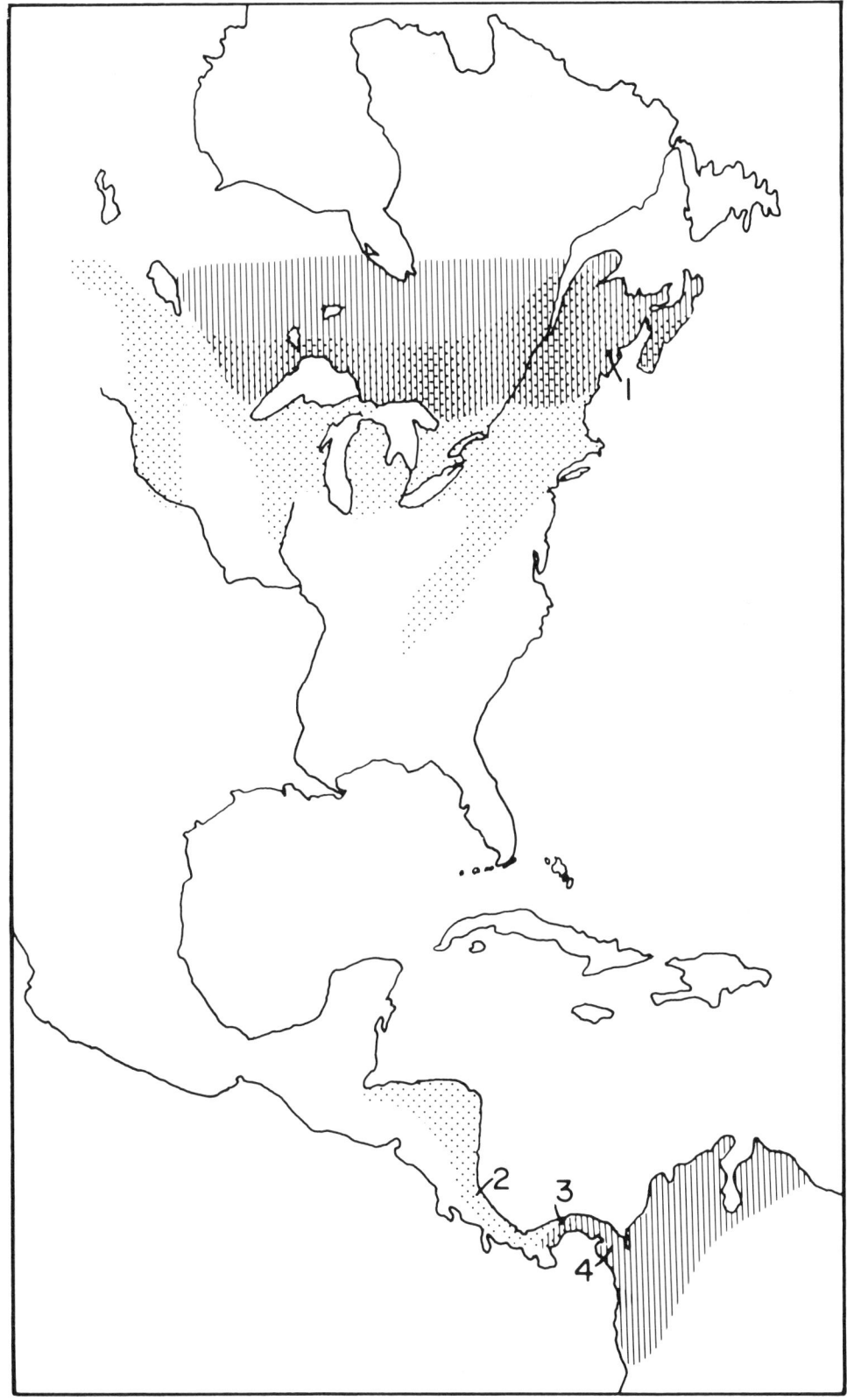

FIG. 1. The breeding and wintering ranges of Bay-breasted (lined) and Chestnut-sided (stippled) warblers. The major study sites are indicated by the following numbers: (1) Maine; (2) La Selva; (3) Canal Zone; (4) Darien.

WINTER DISTRIBUTIONS

The winter ranges of Bay-breasted and Chestnut-sided warblers overlap only narrowly in the region of the Panama Canal Area. The Bay-breasted Warbler is found primarily in northwestern South America and the Chestnut-sided Warbler is characteristic of nuclear Central America. The Bay-breasted Warbler is probably rare in Costa Rica (Slud 1964) and is unrecorded from the western Panama province of Chiriqui (Eisenmann pers. comm.). While the Chestnut-sided Warbler has been recorded throughout Panama and into Colombia (Ridgely 1976; Meyer de Shaunsee 1970), it is rare, in my experience, in Darien.

Both species probably arrive in Panama via a transgulf route (Eisenmann 1957; Rappole et al. 1980). Both are uncommon northwest of their winter ranges during fall migration. Bay-breasted Warblers arrived in mass migration waves during the last few days of October during both years that I was present on the Isthmus of Panama, giving the impression of a "fall-out" from an over-water flight. The spring migration route is less clear. No mass movements are detectable in the Canal Area. In my experience both species gradually disappear, with locally marked winter residents remaining throughout the species' stay (to late April). The Bay-breasted Warbler is rare in Nicaragua and Costa Rica, so some transgulf movement must occur (Rappole et al. 1980).

MORPHOLOGY

Plumages of Bay-breasted and Chestnut-sided warblers are described and pictured in a variety of sources (Bent 1953; Dwight 1900) and will not be discussed here. I have quantified the overall shape and fine morphology of both species with detailed measurements of formalin-fixed specimens collected in the Canal Area by E. S. Morton. External measurements were taken on the specimens, which were then stripped to obtain skeletal measurements. The measurements (Table 1) suggest that overall body size, as indicated by linear measurements of wing chord, tail length, weight, sternum length, and bony wing length, averages 10-15% greater for the Bay-breasted Warbler. Most variables related to morphological structures of the head, such as skull size, culmen, eye size, and rictal bristle length, are essentially identical for the two species. This indicates that the Chestnut-sided Warbler has, essentially, a Bay-breasted Warbler feeding apparatus mounted on a smaller body. The hyoid and bony lower mandible are two fine structures that are substantially longer in the Bay-breasted Warbler.

Table 1. Measurements of Bay-breasted and Chestnut-sided warblers

Measurement	Chestnut-sided (n = 13) $\bar{X}$	S.E.	Bay-Breasted (n = 21) $\bar{X}$	S.E.	Ratio	p[a]
Weight[b]	8.98 g	(.125)	11.22 g	(.120)	1.07	.001
Sternum length	1.14 cm	(.012)	1.21 cm	(.009)	1.12	.001
Bony wing[c]	2.99	(.040)	3.34	(.020)	1.11	.001
Humerus	1.30	(.015)	1.45	(.009)	1.08	.001
Radius-Ulna	1.72	(.021)	1.92	(.016)	1.12	.001
Wing chord	6.12	(.042)	7.00	(.031)	1.14	.001
Tail	4.39	(.059)	4.78	(.068)	1.16	.001
Tarsus	4.04	(.060)	4.37	(.030)	1.08	.001
Metatarsus	1.67	(.030)	1.78	(.002)	1.06	.001
Tibiatarsus	2.40	(.030)	2.58	(.015)	1.08	.001
Skull length	1.56	(0.15)	1.61	(.009)	1.03	.01
Skull width	1.23	(.013)	1.25	(.007)		n.s.
Skull depth	1.02	(.008)	1.05	(.007)	1.03	.05
Eye size[d]	0.35	(.009)	0.35	(.011)		n.s.
Upper Mandible length[e]	1.14	(.020)	1.21	(.012)	1.06	.005
Culmen (front of nares)	0.77	(.038)	0.77	(0.46)	1.00	n.s.
Gape	1.29	(.053)	1.37	(.060)	1.06	n.s.
Upper mandible width (base)	0.36	(.009)	0.36	(.004)		n.s.
Upper mandible depth (base)	0.40	(.005)	0.40	(.003)		n.s.
Upper mandible width (nares)	0.26	(.005)	0.26	(.004)		n.s.
Upper mandible depth (nares)	0.21	(.005)	0.21	(.003)		n.s.
Gape width[e]	0.68	(0.20)	0.70	(.008)		n.s.
Tongue pad length	0.91	(.014)	0.93	(.011)		n.s.
Tongue pad width	0.205	(.005)	0.22	(.005)	1.07	.05
Hyoid length	1.49	(.029)	1.60	(.023)	1.07	.01

a. t-test.
b. Ratio based on cube root of body weights.
c. Radius-ulna + Humerus.
d. The product of the width and depth of eye balls freshly dissected from alcoholic specimens. Since the tissue was firmly attached to orbital, little shrinkage occurred.
e. Skeletal measurements.

STUDY SITES

WINTER SEASON STUDY SITES

I observed warblers in Panama during the periods of 1 December 1976 to 6 January 1977, 13 October 1977 to 21 March 1978, and 20 October 1978 to 1 May 1979. I continued to study resident foliage-gleaning birds from 1 May to 10 September 1979 and from 18 July to 16 September 1980 (Fig. 2). The bulk of my field work was conducted on Barro Colorado Island (BCI) in the Panama Canal (9°09'N, 79°51'W). The island, a hilltop in the Chagres River Valley before Gatun Lake was formed in 1914, is covered with moist lowland forest (Holderidge 1967), receiving on the average approximately 2500 mm rain annually (Fig.3). The vegetation, geology, and avifauna are thoroughly discussed in Croat (1978), Knight (1975), and Willis and Eisenmann (1979).

Outside of a small (0.8 ha) laboratory clearing, the entire island is forested. Roughly 40% of the forest is "old forest," structurally mature (90-120 foot canopy), but of unknown age. The rest of the island is old secondary forest (60-90 foot canopy) less than 100 years old, which was farmland or young forest when the island reserve was established in 1924 (Croat 1978). The forest itself is a mosaic of patches of varying ages (Hartshorne 1978). This patchiness results from local disturbances caused by the death of large canopy trees or the clearing of larger areas in intense wind storms.

The rainfall on the Isthmus of Panama is distinctly seasonal. Barro Colorado Island experiences an annual dry season, averaging less than 10 cm of rain per month, that usually lasts from December to May (Fig. 3). Most of the rain falls during the wet season from May to December. This is the average duration of seasons, but average seasons are rare. During the five years prior to this study, dry seasons have lasted three to six months. During the three winters that I observed warblers, the dry season began at the end of November or early December (Fig. 2). The dry season is characterized by strong (10-15 km) northeasterly trade winds. These winds, which are strongest in the afternoons, subside in March or April. During the rainy season, temperatures are somewhat lower and heavy winds are associated only with local convection storms. Rainfall during the wet season can be intense but is generally of short duration.

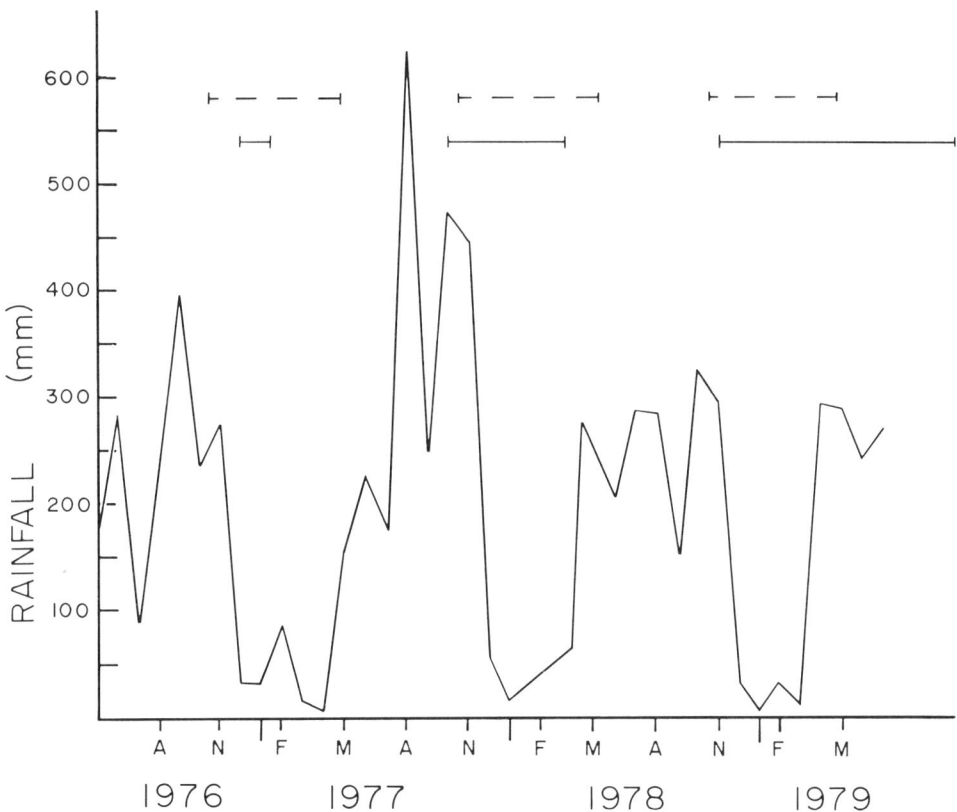

FIG. 2. Monthly rainfall on BCI (Environmental Studies Program data) during the course of the study. Also indicated is the approximate stay of Bay-breasted and Chestnut-sided warblers (dashed line) and stay of the author (solid).

Barro Colorado Island was selected as a primary study site because the 40 km trail system provides access to 1500 ha of forest. Other areas in the Canal Area with extensive moist forest are generally inaccessible except by wading up major streams. I believe that it is important to study these warblers in forested rather than more disturbed habitats since Central America was presumably largely forested in recent geological history (Bennett 1968). In addition, the warblers can be observed to select from a more diverse array of food plants and to associate and interact with a larger pool of resident species.

Barro Colorado Island has an avifauna that is depauperate and somewhat different from equivalent mainland sites (Willis 1974; Willis and Eisenmann 1979). This should not affect the conclusions of this study for several reasons. Most of the potential competitors of *Dendroica* can be found on BCI. The island has a nearly complete canopy avifauna (Greenberg 1981c), and few species of mid-level foliage gleaners are missing. The mixed species flocks on BCI are similar to antwren flocks that I have observed in exposed ridge tops in the Pipeline Road forest of the adjacent mainland. What appears to be missing are those species

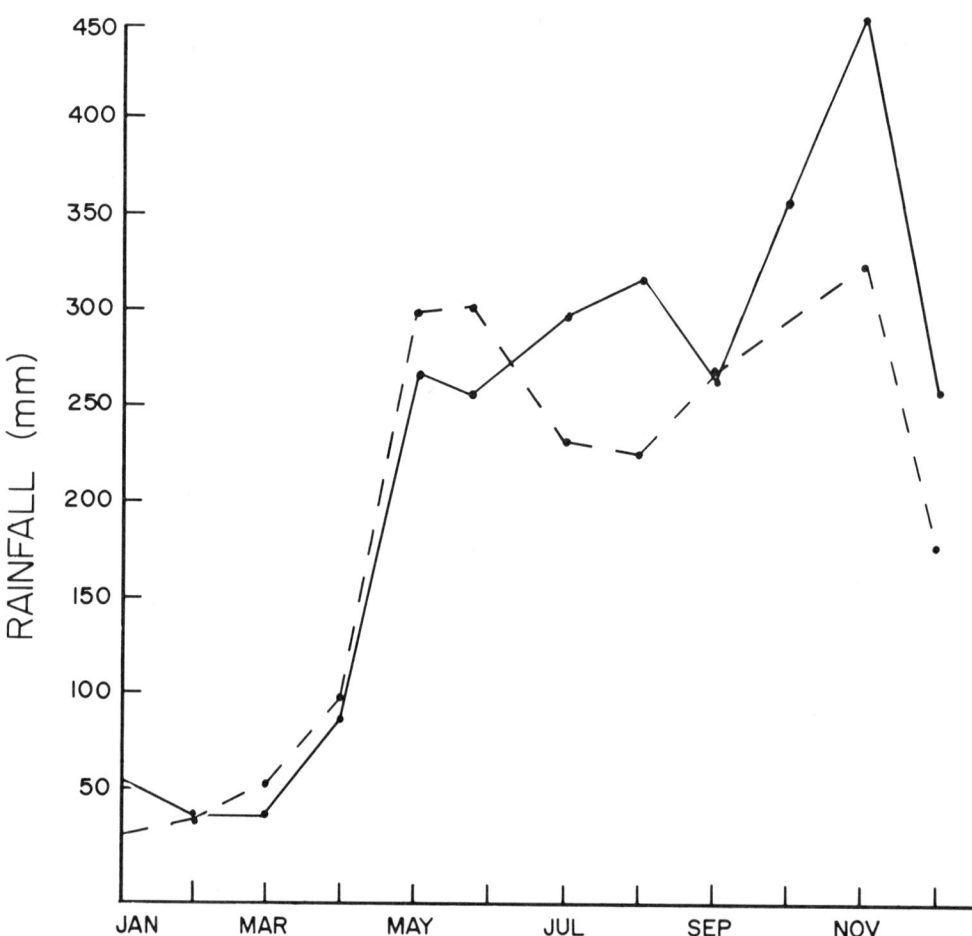

FIG. 3. Mean monthly rainfall for BCI (solid line, from Ridgely 1976) and Boca de Cupa Darien Province, Panama (dashed line, IRHE data).

associated with low wet areas along permanent streams such as Rio Frijoles. Flocks that have a nucleus including *Chlorothraupis carmioli*, *Hylophilus ochraceiceps*, and *Thamnistes anabatinus* may not be found on BCI because such low wet areas are scarce.

Moreover, differences in the BCI avifauna are not a critical problem for this study since I am comparing the behavior of two species of migrants, rather than studying the competitive interactions of migrants and residents. Bay-breasted and Chestnut-sided warblers are responding to the same available resources, the same forest phenology, and the same array of ecologically similar species. Further, I have made observations at a number of off-island sites to establish the generality of the patterns that I have quantitatively determined on BCI.

I observed and censused warblers at other Canal Area localities. The Isthmus of Panama provides a sharp moisture gradient from the wet Caribbean slope to the dry Pacific coast (Ridgely 1976). I visited the following sites in Central Panama (listed from wet to dry with approximate annual rainfall and the number of visits in parentheses):

Achiote Road-Fort Sherman (3500 mm, 4). Young second-growth forest.

Pipeline Road (2500-3000 mm, 12). Most of the observations were made along the major streams that drain into Gatun Lake (formerly Chagres River). These include Rio Frijoles, Rio Limbo, Rio Mendoza, Rio Agua Salud.

Frijoles Road (2500 mm, 12). Young second-growth scrub and forest along small road from Frijoles to Pipeline Road (see census route description).

Madden Forest Reserve (2000 mm, 4). An area of young second-growth forest along the Las Cruces Trail.

Paraiso (1700 mm, 11). Young second growth forest and grassland along the continental divide (Gold Hill, see census route description).

Chiva Chiva Road (1700 mm, 4). Young secondary forest.

Farfan Road (1500 mm, 2). Young secondary forest and scrub.

I also observed Bay-breasted Warblers during three week-long expeditions to the Cerro Pirre region of Darien (180 km SE Panama City; 8°03'N, 77°44'W). I visited the area with J. Gradwohl on 15-22 February 1978, 18-24 December 1978, and 11-17 February 1979. The climate of lowland Darien, along the Rio Tuire is similar to central Panama (Fig. 3). While rainfall patterns of BCI and Boca de Cupa (15 km SE El Real on Rio Tuire) are very similar, the El Real area apparently lacks the strong consistent trade winds during the dry season and, perhaps as a result, the canopy is less deciduous.

Rio Pirre winds through agricultural fields and small patches of secondary forest with occasional large trees, particularly *Anacardium excelsum*. Common trees of the second growth are similar to those found in the Canal Area (*Trema micrantha*, *Spondias*, *Ficus*, *Xylopia frutescens*) with some notable exceptions; *Miconia argentea* and *Didymopanax morototoni*, both important food trees for small birds in the Canal Area (Morton 1980; A. Worthington pers. comm.; this study), were not observed in the Pirre Region although they apparently occur (Croat 1978). From the Choco village of Pijibasal upstream to Dos Bocas, patches of forest become larger and more mature. Trails wind up the narrow spur ridges from Pijibasal to the summit of Cerro Pirre, which is usually enshrouded. Within a day's walk, the trail passes through mature lowland forest into elfin cloud forest at the ridge top.

I visited Finca La Selva near Puerto Viejo, on the Caribbean slope of Costa Rica, for five days in January 1978. The bird life and vegetation of this area are well described by Slud (1960). The 790 ha reserve contains both second growth and mature lowland tropical wet forest (3900 mm).

FOREST PHENOLOGY ON BARRO COLORADO ISLAND

The seasonality in rainfall on Barro Colorado Island is strongly reflected in the availability of food for foraging birds. Fruit, particularly of canopy and subcanopy trees, displays strong peaks (Croat 1978; Foster 1973; Leigh and Smythe 1979) of abundance in the late dry to early wet season (March-June). Fruit is particularly scarce in the canopy during the late wet season (October-December). These peaks and valleys in general fruit production may not accurately reflect the seasonality of fruit used by warblers since warblers use only a fraction of the species of bird-dispersed fruit (Greenberg 1981a).

Arthropod abundance is also highly seasonal; insects respond to the leaf flush associated with the beginning of the rainy season (Wolda 1978). The canopy is semi-deciduous, with many trees losing their foliage in the dry season. Insects also increase as the leaf litter and other decaying material becomes moist (Gradwohl and Greenberg 1983; Willis 1976).

To obtain a more refined picture of the seasonal pattern of abundance in foliage arthropods, I directly censused understory shrubs (see Greenberg and Gradwohl 1980). These census data provide the number of arthropods per 10,000 leaves. The standing crop of leaves is, however, seasonally variable (Leigh and Smythe 1979). To correct for this variation, I counted the number of leaves on 50 marked shrubs in February (dry season), June (wet season), and August (wet season). The estimated number of arthropods per ten thousand leaves weighted by the relative abundance of leaves in that season is presented in Fig. 4. The nadir for total arthropods was in the late wet, early dry, and late dry season. The seasonal fluctuation in numbers was not great. The number of large arthropods (> 1.0 cm) showed a severe seasonal depression during the late dry season. However, these direct censuses may obscure an important pattern of seasonality. Orthoptera appear to be important breeding resources for antwrens and other foliage-gleaning birds (Gradwohl and Greenberg 1983; Greenberg 1981b). While my direct censuses were relatively inefficient at detecting large numbers of orthopterans, light-trap data (from the Smithsonian Environmental Sciences Program) indicate extreme seasonality in capture rate of orthopterans (Gradwohl and Greenberg 1983), with large orthopterans nearly absent in the early to mid dry season. Migrants are present during a period of low abundance of arthropods, particularly large arthropods. Resident foliage gleaners breed primarily during the wet season (Willis and Eisenmann 1979; Gradwohl and Greenberg 1983) when large Orthoptera are common.

BREEDING SEASON STUDY SITES

I studied the foraging behavior of Chestnut-sided and Bay-breasted warblers on their breeding grounds in Maine from 5 June to 17 July of 1980. The Chestnut-sided Warbler was observed primarily on the campus of the University of Maine, Orono, in an area of young deciduous scrub west of the playing fields. This 2 ha area was covered with willows (*Salix* sp.), alder (*Alnus* sp.), Gray Birch (*Betula populifolia*), and Quaking Aspen (*Populus tremuloides*) and bounded a plot of young deciduous forest with Red Maple (*Acer rubrum*), Gray Birch, American Beech (*Fagus grandifolia*), and some White Spruce (*Picea glauca*), Balsam Fir (*Abies balsamea*), and Tamarack (*Larix laricina*). Bay-breasted Warblers were observed mainly at Nesowadnehunk Creek Campground in Baxter State Park. This area, as well as most of the spruce-fir vegetation in northern Maine and eastern Canada, was under siege from Spruce Budworm (*Chirostoneura fumiferana*) during

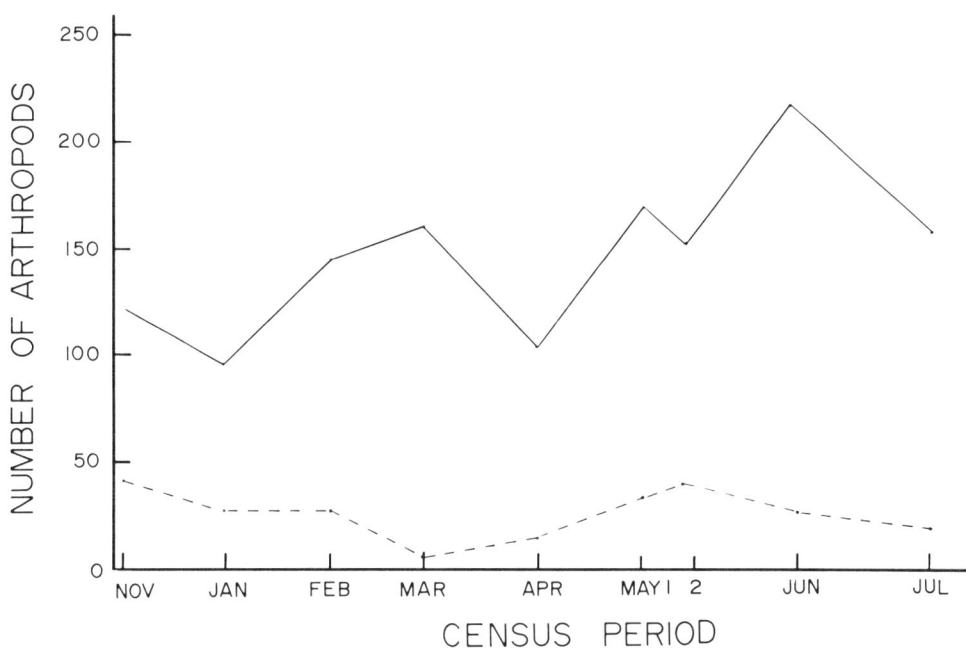

FIG. 4. Number of arthropods (solid line) and large arthropods (> 10 mm, dashed line) per 10,000 leaves censused in the understory of the BCI forest (see Greenberg and Gradwohl 1980); numbers are weighted by the relative standing crop of leaves on 50 marked shrubs. May-June census data were multiplied by 1.28 and August data by 0.89 because there were 1.28 and 0.89 times as many leaves/shrub or sapling during June and August as in February. The November census results are unweighted since no leaf abundance census was conducted. The rainy season is indicated with a dotted line.

the course of this study (Jones 1980). This campground lies at a major ecotone between mixed-conifer deciduous forest and solid spruce-fir forest (to the north). I worked in an area intermingled with spruce-fir and alder thickets. I spent 13 days on the Bay-breasted Warbler study site between 18 June and 8 July; I worked 20 days on the primary study site for the Chestnut-sided Warbler (5 June - 15 July). Bay-breasted Warblers were also observed at Pleasant Lake, Washington County, in a small patch of spruce-fir and Eastern Hemlock (*Tsuga canadensis*) on 11 June. Chestnut-sided Warblers were watched in an area of alder, willow, and Red Maple scrub at the edge of the Stillwater Bog, near Bangor.

In addition to observations of foraging Bay-breasted Warblers, I also gathered data on several other breeding *Dendroica* including Myrtle, Magnolia, Palm, and Yellow warblers. Data on Myrtle and Magnolia warblers were taken from the same areas where I observed Bay-breasted Warblers. Yellow Warblers were studied at the sites for Chestnut-sided Warblers. Palm Warblers, however, were found in the Tamarack and Black Spruce (*Picea mariana*) thickets in the center of the Stillwater Bog.

METHODS

I employed a large number of techniques to quantify various aspects of the winter exploitation systems of Bay-breasted and Chestnut-sided warblers. Major methods will be outlined below; other less frequently used techniques will be discussed within the Results sections.

POPULATION DENSITY

Since both species of *Dendroica* are common at mid- to high levels in the forest, I censused warblers by counting birds heard or seen. Censuses were conducted along 1 km transects and birds located within 15 m of each side of the trail were tallied. The area censused was approximately 3 ha and census results will be presented as densities. Censuses were conducted in the morning (0630-1030) for 90-150 minutes. I walked slowly along the trail, pausing to listen for warbler call notes. My constant progress was interrupted to count the members of mixed-species flocks encountered within the transect boundaries upon location of the flock. Censuses along BCI trails were conducted at least three to four times each month and were spaced, as weather allowed, at even intervals; postponements of two to three days occurred during particularly windy periods of the dry season. Individuals of all bird species were recorded. I noted the location of all bird sightings within 50 m segments of the transect. Differential detectability of bird species is undoubtedly a problem with this, as well as all other methods of censusing tropical forest birds. Shy understory birds may easily escape detection; high canopy birds may also be undercounted. This census technique is best suited for estimating the densities of mid-level insectivorous birds, such as warblers, greenlets, and antwrens. The following is a description of the transects censuses on BCI and other areas.

Snyder-Molino: I censused this BCI trail in December 1977 (seven censuses), October 1977 to March 1978 (23), and November 1978 to April 1979 (20). The trail winds along ridge tops through young forest for 600 m, passes through scrubby young forest on an old plantation site for 200 m, and skirts patches of old forest for 200 m.

Wheeler: I censused this transect October 1977 to March 1978 (23) and November 1978 to April 1979 (21). This section of Wheeler trail (from signpost 12 to 22) runs along the edge of the central plateau on BCI, passing through 300 m of young forest and 700 m of old forest. The old forest has several large areas of local disturbance including two major gap systems (one created by a lightning strike) and 150 m of blow-down (about 25 years old).

Barbour: I censused this trail in December 1977 (6) and December 1978 (3). This route passes along the rim of Lutz ravine (600 m) and through low flat terrain (400 m), winding entirely through young forest.

Frijoles Road: This transect runs along a small dirt track that begins at Frijoles on the northeastern shore of Gatun Lake (opposite BCI) and ends at Pipeline Road. The road runs along a ridge top with young (approximately 20 year old) vegetation and is surrounded by young forest on the slopes of deep ravines. Some of the common trees include the dominant second growth plants of the Canal Area: *Cecropia*, *Didymopanax morototoni*, *Luehea seemannii*, *Miconia argentea*, *Pseudobombax septenatum*, *Spondias*, *Trema micrantha*, *Trichospermum mexicanum*, and *Xylopia frutescens*.

Paraiso: A census was conducted on the road system near the continental divide near Gold Hill. The area has islands of scrubby woodland, with many typically dry forest tree species (*Enterilobium*, *Bursera simaruba*, etc.) surrounded by a sea of tall grassland. Three hundred meters of the transect passed through moist forest on the slopes of Gold Hill having many of the same plant species that are found on BCI (*Gustavia superba*, *Pseudobombax septenatum*, *Spondias*). While lacking *Miconia argentea*, many of the trees were the same common second-growth species that I found on the Frijoles Road transect. In addition, both of these second-growth study sites had large patches of *Heliconia lathispatha* which supported large hummingbird and honeycreeper populations in the late wet season.

GROUP SIZE

I recorded the group size of all warblers observed on each study site, including BCI, other Canal Zone localities, La Selva, and the Pirre region. Warbler flocks are often loose in structure, so I included as part of a group the maximum number of birds that were observed within a 20 m diameter circle.

SPACING SYSTEM

I based my inferences of spacing systems on a small number of marked or individually recognizable warblers on BCI. Six Bay-breasted Warblers were color-banded in the BCI forest and ten in the laboratory clearing. Chestnut-sided Warblers were only color-banded in the clearing (n = 4), but others were often individually recognizable throughout entire winters (until prenuptial molt) by distinct plumage characteristics. These included the presence, size, and shape of chestnut side markings, presence of yellow on vent, and distribution of residual facial markings. Bay-breasted Warblers were also variable in plumage, and several individuals could be recognized, but usually the markings were graded (brightness of buff or rufous) and difficult to distinguish. Several Magnolia Warblers were recognized by banding (1) or plumage characteristics (2). I focused my attention on a 6-ha study area on the central plateau of BCI for most of my resighting efforts. This is the area that was used in a study of spacing systems and flocking behavior of resident birds (Gradwohl and Greenberg 1980).

MIXED-SPECIES FLOCKING

Judy Gradwohl and I kept a record of the species composition of all mixed-species flocks that we encountered on walks through the BCI forest. We hiked all 40 km of trails during the two winters of flock censusing, but several trails (Armour, Conrad, Lake, Miller, Snyder-Molino, Wheeler, Zetek) were walked more frequently and a few trails (Gross, Wetmore) were censused rarely. A flock was defined as an association of birds within a 20 m diameter, and, as much as possible, a mental circle was drawn to include the maximum number of birds. While the same stretch of trail was censused on different days, flock formation is sufficiently dynamic in one area (Gradwohl and Greenberg 1980) so that each census can probably be considered independent. Since most residents occur solitarily or in small family groups, and it is difficult to estimate the numbers of all flock species, I use the number of resident species instead of individuals in my analyses.

For every warbler I observed on BCI, I recorded whether it was associated in a mixed-species group, including aggregations visiting fruiting or flowering trees. Close associations between warblers and other species were quantified by recording the birds present within 5 m of a focal warbler selected for foraging observations (see Foraging Microhabitat). The persistence of individual warblers in following antwren groups was investigated with Gradwohl and some data have been published (Gradwohl and Greenberg 1980).

FORAGING MICROHABITAT

During the winter of 1977-1978 I recorded the estimated foraging height of all warblers encountered in the BCI forest. For the entire study I recorded the foraging microhabitat and attack behavior of warblers selected on predesignated transects through the BCI forest. During these transects efforts were made to observe all warblers and not just the most easily located individuals. Some bias against birds high in the canopy is inevitable since they are more difficult to locate from the ground. To minimize the bias, foraging height was recorded even if other foraging observations could not be made. Inability to locate higher birds is difficult to assess, but the bias should be towards an overestimate of the similarity of foraging height distributions when comparing high and low foraging species. In no case was the first foraging maneuver recorded since this would have biased my sample towards more conspicuous foraging tactics (e.g., hover gleaning versus simple gleaning). If a group of warblers was encountered I took foraging data on one of every three individuals. Some bias against flocking birds is inherent in the data. Group size was generally small and this bias was probably trivial.

Variables I recorded from selected birds include those describing foraging location, foraging substrate, and foraging tactics (Table 2). Foraging height, canopy height, and tree height were estimated; estimates were periodically checked against readings through a 200 mm telephoto lens. Heights were analyzed

Table 2. Foraging variables recorded from *Dendroica* and other foliage-gleaning birds

Variable	Example or definition
Forest type	Old or young forest
Canopy height (ft)	
Tree height (ft)	
Foraging height (ft)	
Plant type	Tree, understory shrub, vine
Leaf size	Estimated length and width of leaf of plant in which bird perched
Diameter of perch branch (cm)	
Crown cover over bird	Estimated percent within one meter of bird

Foraging substrate	Live leaf
	  upper surface
	  lower surface
	Dead leaf
	Twig
	Branch
	Trunk
	Flower
	Fruit

Foraging attack method	Glean (body stationary) Leap (upward movement) Hover (upward movement, bird remains stationary by rapid wing movement) Lunge (level or downward movement) Dart (aerial attack, bird continues in same direction) Sally (aerial attack, bird returns to original position) Hang (bird leaps and grabs on to under surface Lean (bird leans over and hangs on to under surface
Attack distance (ft)	

by broad strata so a 10 percent error in estimates should not greatly affect the results. Leaf size, branch diameter, and attack distances were also estimated.

To compare the foraging behavior of Bay-breasted and Chestnut-sided warblers with resident foliage-gleaners, I gathered similar data for several common "warbler-like" birds in the BCI forest. These species are largely insectivorous, relatively small bodied, and move about actively in search of foliage insects. The resident species include the antwrens, *Myrmotherula axillaris* and *Microrhopias quixensis*, the greenlet *Hylophilus decurtatus*, and the small omnivorous tanagers *Dacnis cayana* and *Tachyphonus luctuosus*.

I examined the leaf arrangements on the branches used by foraging birds (1978-1979). I classified foliage arrangements in 6 basic types, which were further lumped into four major classes for most of the analyses:

Planar—Branches are oriented more or less horizontally, leaves are curled or arranged on the same horizontal plane.
Semiplanar—Branches are oriented horizontally, leaves are curled or angled upward or downward from the horizontal planes.
Orthotropic tree—Branches are associated with shrub or tree and oriented more than 30 degrees from horizontal; leaves are arranged at oblique angles to branch.
Clustered tree—A tuft of leaves originates at terminal end of branch or stem.
Palm—Foliage associated with palms.
Orthotropic vine—Vines climb in non-horizontal direction; leaves are arranged obliquely or planar to this axis.

The major classes include palm, orthotropic (including clustered) tree, orthotropic vine, and planar (semiplanar or planar, vine or tree). I recorded leaf arrangements for the first branch on which a foraging bird was observed. Available foliage was censused along six trail sections (two in old and four in young forest). I selected 25 random points within 10 m of each trail (150 points). At each point I recorded the number, height, and type of branches intersecting an imaginary line through the center of a narrow tube.

FORAGING MOVEMENT PATTERNS

I recorded on cassette tape the type and distance of movements of 32 foraging Chestnut-sided (6030 sec.) and 30 Bay-breasted warblers (5020 sec.) during three sampling periods 1977-1979. Movements were classified into those that involve changing branches or branch systems (hops and flights) and those that involve movement along a branch (< 4 inches, short creep; > 4 inches, long creep). All attempted foraging motions were recorded as well. Many short sequences were taken because warblers are hard to follow for long periods in tropical forests. Inter-individual variability can be calculated on the basis of many small samples. I employed nonparametric tests using mean values for each sequence as single observations to test for interspecific differences.

FRUGIVORY

Observations of warblers at fruiting trees are fully described in Greenberg (1981a). I base my estimates of the number of visits to *Miconia* trees on the observations of marked individuals in the BCI clearing. Nutritional analysis of fruit was conducted by the University of Alaska Agricultural Research Laboratory. The analyses included tests for total nonstructural carbohydrates, crude fat, and nitrogen.

BREEDING FORAGING BEHAVIOR

I continuously recorded (on cassettes) movements and foraging tactics of warblers selected as I walked through breeding habitat. I moved slowly and stealthily, attempting to locate cryptically foraging individuals. Still, I had an unavoidable bias towards observations of males, the more conspicuous sex during early nesting activities. I avoided taking data from males that were not actively foraging; sequences in which birds paused for longer than 30 seconds were not analyzed. The motivation of foraging birds presumably varies considerably with sex, time of day, and other variables related to intensity of territorial maintenance. Because of this, the absolute rates of various activities are not comparable with nonbreeding foraging data. The primary basis of comparison is the relative frequency of different kinds of movements. All foraging maneuvers were taken from transcripts of these tapes; data include foraging substrate and attack method. I also recorded locomotor data similar to those taken on wintering warblers. I summed the estimated distances of individual motions to determine the relative distances moved by different movement types. Since males frequently flew long distances for territorial maintenance, flights of over 15 feet were not included. To locate birds with respect to surrounding foliage, 30 seconds into each foraging bout, I estimated the distance of the nearest foliage directly overhead and on the same branch (or horizontal plane if branch was vertically oriented).

ABUNDANCE, HABITAT DISTRIBUTION, AND MOVEMENTS OF WARBLERS

ABUNDANCE OF BAY-BREASTED AND CHESTNUT-SIDED WARBLERS

Bay-breasted and Chestnut-sided warblers are the most common wood warblers in the woodlands and forests of the Canal Area during the winter (also see Eisenmann 1957; Hespenheide 1980; Morton 1980). On Barro Colorado Island (BCI), I found Bay-breasted Warblers in average densities (over 3 winters and 2 forest types) of 1.3/ha; Chestnut-sided Warblers were considerably less common (0.3/ha). The greater abundance of Bay-breasted over Chestnut-sided Warblers was consistent over all localities and several years of observation in the Canal Area (Table 3). In fact, the Bay-breasted Warbler was generally four times more common than the Chestnut-sided Warbler at my census sites (range = 2-7:1). Most other workers have reported the numerical dominance of the Bay-breasted Warbler in the Canal Area. Willis (1966, 1980) ranked the Bay-breasted Warbler as somewhat more common than the Chestnut-sided Warbler based on his 10 years of field work on BCI. Morton (1980) and Hespenheide (1980) found Bay-breasted Warblers to be more common along transects located throughout the Isthmus. Eisenmann (pers. comm.), however, believed that Chestnut-sided Warblers outnumbered Bay-breasted Warblers in the Canal Area. This might be because of his greater concentration on scrubby habitats. On the other hand, given the potential for long-term population fluctuations, particularly in Bay-breasted Warblers responding to recent (Jones 1980) Spruce Budworm outbreaks, changes in the relative abundances of these species would not be surprising.

HABITAT DISTRIBUTION OF WARBLERS

I found Bay-breasted Warblers to be more common in old forest than in young forest on BCI. Bay-breasted Warblers were found at overall densities of 1.6/ha along the Wheeler transect and at only 1.0/ha along the Snyder-Molino transect; a two-way analysis of variance (ANOVA: habitat versus season) indicated this habitat difference was nearly significant (F = 2.97, d.f. = 1,74, p < .10). The Chestnut-sided Warbler was found at approximately equal densities in the two forest types. Willis (1980) suggested that all species of migrants were more common in young rather than old forest. I found the converse to be true of Bay-breasted Warblers, but patchy distribution of migrants may make subjective

Table 3. The density of Bay-breasted and Chestnut-sided warblers on transect censuses

Transect	Year	N[a]	Early BBW	Early CSW	Late BBW	Late CSW	Total[b] BBW	Total[b] CSW
Snyder-Molino	1976	7, 0	8.0	2.0			8.0	2.0
	1977	9, 11	2.4 (0.4)[c]	1.7 (0.5)	1.7 (0.5)	0.6 (0.2)	1.9	0.6
	1978	9, 14	6.4 (1.5)	1.1 (0.4)	2.8 (0.5)	0.8 (0.3)	4.6	0.9
Total[d]							3.3	0.8
Wheeler	1977	9, 12	4.8 (1.1)	0.6 (0.2)	2.0 (1.1)	0.5 (0.2)	3.4	0.6
	1978	9, 14	10.6 (1.3)	2.3 (0.5)	1.4 (1.0)	1.4 (0.3)	6.0	1.9
Total							4.7	1.3
Barbour	1976	6, 0	9.8 (1.3)	2.9 (0.3)			9.8	2.9
Paraiso	1977	6, 4	7.0 (1.1)	3.0 (0.3)	1.8 (0.9)	1.6 (0.7)	4.4	2.3
Frijoles	1977	5, 4	7.0 (1.6)	1.3 (0.3)	5.0 (1.9)	1.3 (0.3)	6.0	1.3

a. Number of censuses per period (early, late).
b. Mean of period means (early + late)/2.
c. Mean with standard error in parentheses.
d. Mean of the yearly means (Total 1977 + Total 1978)/2.

estimates difficult. Also, *Dendroica* warblers were most often associated with disturbances within older forest. Neither species was found in much greater density in scrub habitats. While the census data are probably not comparable between forest and scrub habitats because of differential detectability, the Bay-breasted Warbler was only slightly more common along the Paraiso and Frijoles transects when compared to BCI transects the same year (1.8-2.0/ha, see Table 3). The Chestnut-sided Warbler occurred in similar densities in scrub and forest habitats.

SEASONAL AND ANNUAL VARIATION IN WARBLER ABUNDANCE

Both Bay-breasted and Chestnut-sided warblers were more common during 1978-1979 than 1977-1978 (ANOVA: year versus season, CSW $F = 17.9$, d.f. $= 1, 74$, $p < .001$; BBW $F = 2.48$, n.s.) and were more common on BCI transects in December 1976 than in the two following Decembers. Interannual variation in abundance is correlated between species, which suggests, since the species breed in different habitats, that it may be the wintering ground, rather than the breeding ground factors, that have the greatest influence on densities of warblers on BCI. Since annual differences in density can be detected in November and December, the difference may reflect late rainy season conditions in Central America.

The Bay-breasted Warbler showed a consistent seasonal pattern in abundance (ANOVA: seasonal versus annual, $F = 30.1$, $p < .001$). In both years, and on all transects, more Bay-breasted Warblers were observed during early (October-December) than late winter (January-April). Much of this seasonality results from a strong influx in November, which dissipates by mid-December. This is presumably some sort of slow migratory movement. Bay-breasted Warblers disappeared entirely from the driest areas (Paraiso, Chiva Chiva), a phenomenon reported by Morton (1980). In contrast, Chestnut-sided Warblers appeared in low but constant densities in late October and remained in such densities in all areas throughout the winter. Slight decreases in census numbers in late winter were not significant.

RELATIVE ABUNDANCE OF WARBLERS AND RESIDENT FOLIAGE GLEANERS

I found the Bay-breasted Warbler to be the most common foliage-gleaning bird during the winter in most habitats I censused or visited in lowland Panama (Table 4). On the BCI forest transects, *Thamnophilus punctatus*, *Microrhopias* and *Hylophilus decurtatus* were nearly as numerous. When total biomass is considered, the Bay-breasted Warbler falls below *Thamnophilus*. The numerical dominance of the Bay-breasted Warbler is particularly striking in the scrub habitats and outer canopy of the BCI forest (Greenberg 1981c). In these habitats, the next most common foliage-gleaner (*Dacnis cayana*) is less than half as abundant as the Bay-breasted Warbler. The Chestnut-sided Warbler was generally the fourth to sixth most common foliage-gleaning species.

The abundance of the Bay-breasted Warbler has not been widely acknowledged. Karr (1976), for example, recorded it only in October on two of his eight Panamanian study sites. Since he overlooked the most common migrant species, it is not surprising that he concludes "that migrants make up no more than 1-3% of the lowland forest densities [of birds]." Willis (1980) is more generous in his estimates of 0.4/ha Bay-breasted Warblers in the BCI forest. Still, he estimated the Bay-breasted Warbler to have been the fifth most common foliage-gleaning species; he further concluded that no migrant species approached the most common resident species in abundance. In fact, there is no correlation between our rankings of the nine most common foliage-gleaning birds. At this point it is hard to discern whether differences reflect real changes in the avifauna or differences in censusing technique.

The Bay-breasted Warbler could be abnormally common on BCI because of the depauperate nature of the island avifauna. BCI, however, has suffered from the extinction of primarily terrestrial or low strata species of forest insectivores. The canopy avifauna is nearly complete when compared to the Pipeline Road avifauna. My impression from visiting areas of Pipeline Road and the Pirre region is that Bay-breasted Warblers are relatively common in the mainland forests as well. The abundance of Bay-breasted Warblers in the outer forest canopy and secondary woodlands of Darien was particularly impressive. I attribute underestimates of their importance to their patchy distribution (see below) and restriction to outer canopy, where only faint chips indicate their presence (see also Morton 1980). It is clear that significant populations winter in moist lowland forest of Panama.

Table 4. The relative density of the most common foliage-gleaners on transects in the Panama Canal Zone

Transect	Species	$\overline{X}$ no./census	Biomass (g)[a]
Snyder-Molino (43 censuses)	Bay-breasted Warbler	3.3	40
	Microrhopias quixensis	3.1	25
	Hylophilus decurtatus	2.9	26
	Thamnophilus punctatus	2.8	67
	Tachyphonus luctuosus	1.2	16
	Myrmotherula axillaris	1.0	8
	Chestnut-sided Warbler	0.8	7
	Dacnis cayana	0.5	6
Wheeler	Bay-breasted Warbler	4.4	51
	Microrhopias quixensis	4.0	32
	Hylophilus decurtatus	3.6	32
	Thamnophilus punctatus	2.0	48
	Tachyphonus luctuosus	1.8	23
	Myrmotherula axillaris	2.1	17
	Chestnut-sided Warbler	1.2	11
	Dacnis cayana	0.8	10
Paraiso (10 censuses)	Bay-breasted Warbler	4.4	51
	Cyanerpes cyaneus	2.9	51
	Tennessee Warbler	2.7	27
	Chestnut-sided Warbler	2.3	21
	Dacnis cayana	2.2	26
	Hylophilus decurtatus	1.4	13
	Tachyphonus luctuosus	1.1	14
	Thamnophilus doliatus	1.0	25
Frijoles (9 censuses)	Bay-breasted Warbler	6.4	77
	Dacnis cayana	3.1	37
	Tennessee Warbler	3.3	30
	Microrhopias quixensis	2.6	21
	Hylophilus decurtatus	2.1	19
	Myrmotherula axillaris	1.3	10
	Chestnut-sided Warbler	1.2	11

a. Species weight multiplied by $\overline{X}$ no./census (g).

SPATIAL DISTRIBUTION OF WARBLERS IN THE BCI FOREST

The distribution of birds in a lowland tropical forest is far from even. A long silent walk through the forest is occasionally punctuated with the encounter of a large mixed flock. What is perhaps less widely appreciated is that these patches of bird life are often persistent through time. Small areas within the forest tend to be the focal points of most bird activity. The total sightings of Bay-breasted Warblers in each of the 100 × 35 m transect unit (Figs. 5, 6) demonstrate this patchiness. These focal points of activity often persisted between winters, particularly the fifth and sixth unit of the Wheeler transect and the fourth and seventh unit of the Snyder-Molino transect. These areas of high Bay-breasted Warbler density often correspond to good areas for insectivorous birds in general (Fig. 7). The total sightings of Bay-breasted Warblers per transect unit is significantly correlated with

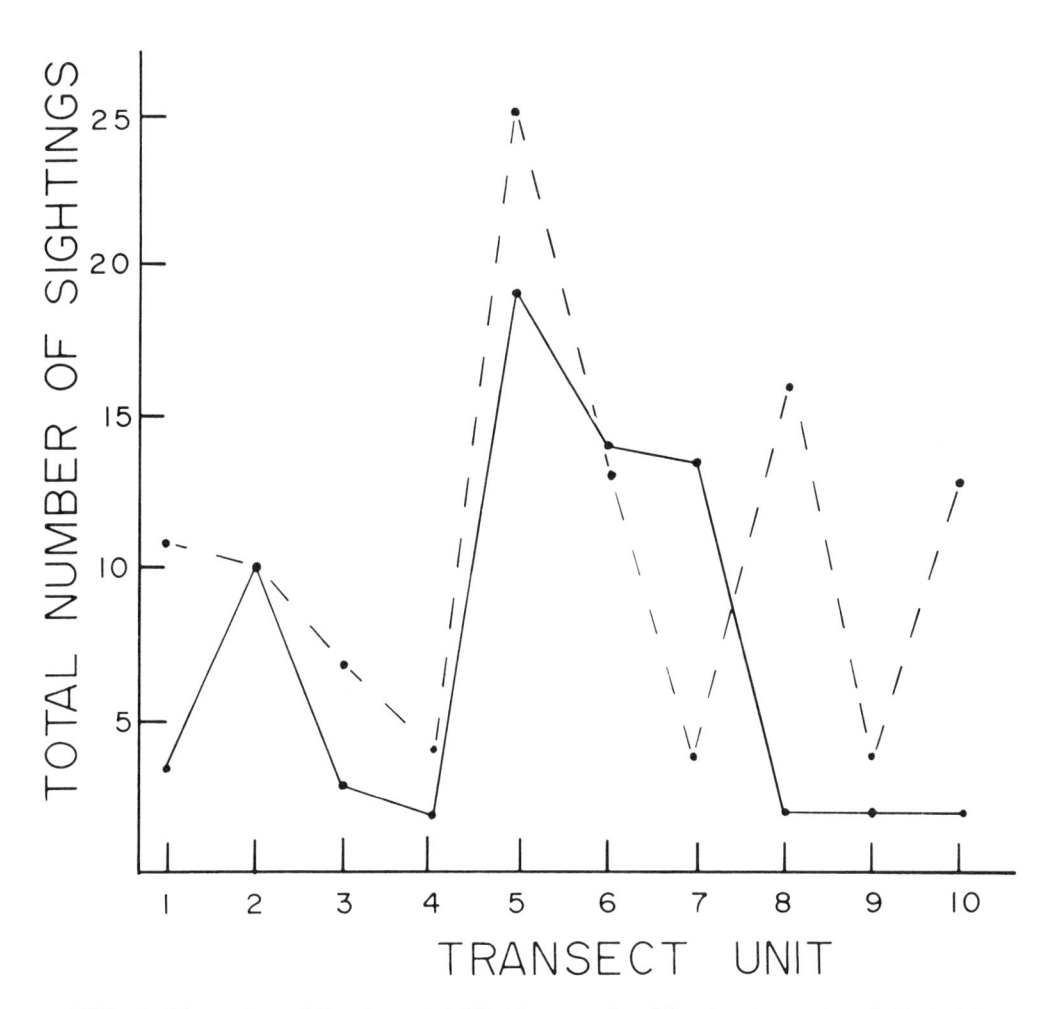

FIG. 5. Dispersion of Bay-breasted Warblers on the Wheeler transect as indicated by the sum of all sightings for each transect unit for each winter (1977-1978 is dashed and 1978-1979 is solid line).

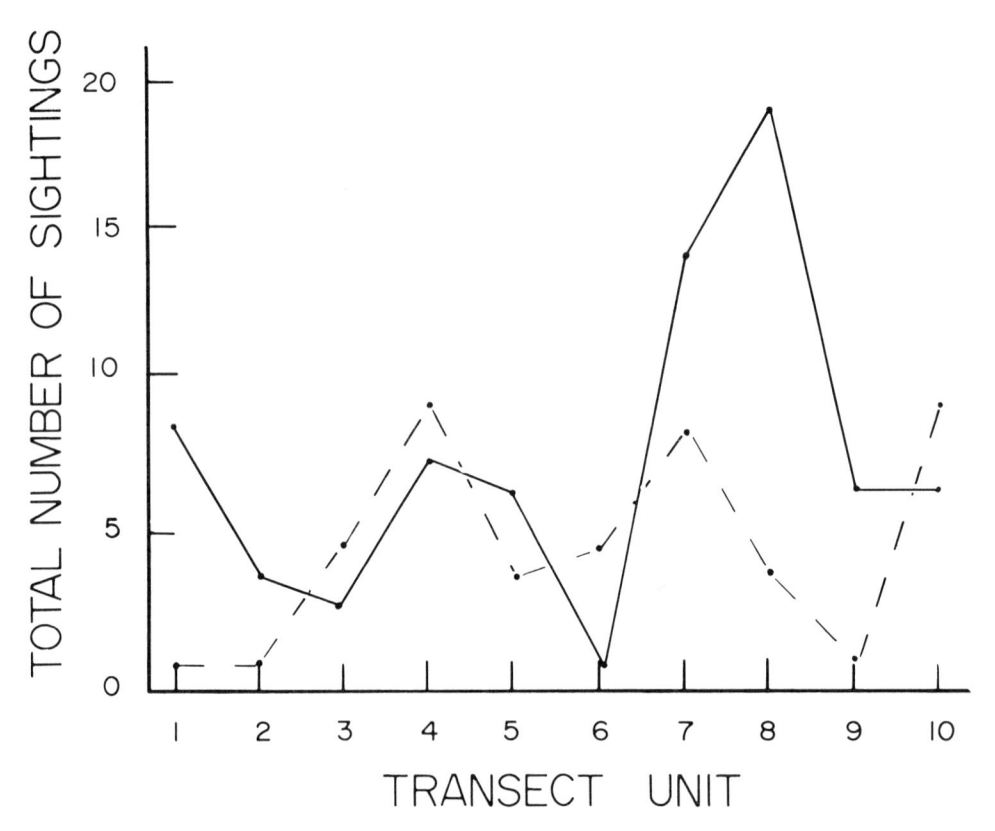

FIG. 6. Dispersion of Bay-breasted Warblers on the Snyder-Molino transect as indicated by the sum of all sightings for each transect unit for each winter (1977-1978 is dashed and 1978-1979 is solid line).

the number of sightings of resident insectivorous birds ($r = .70$, $p < .01$). This correlation is very strong for the Wheeler transect ($r = .84$, $p < .01$) and weak for the Snyder-Molino transect ($r = .32$, n.s.). This difference between the two census routes confirms my subjective impression that both warbler and insectivorous bird distribution is patchier in older forest. Large-scale disturbances within the mature forest are more frequent; whereas, younger forest show a more uniform level of disturbance. This greater amount of habitat heterogeneity and disturbance probably accounts for the greater density of *Dendroica* in the old forest. While these focal points of bird activity tend to be in disturbed areas (i.e., large tree-fall gaps and blow downs), not all such areas had consistently high abundances of birds. Other factors, such as drainage and topography are probably important.

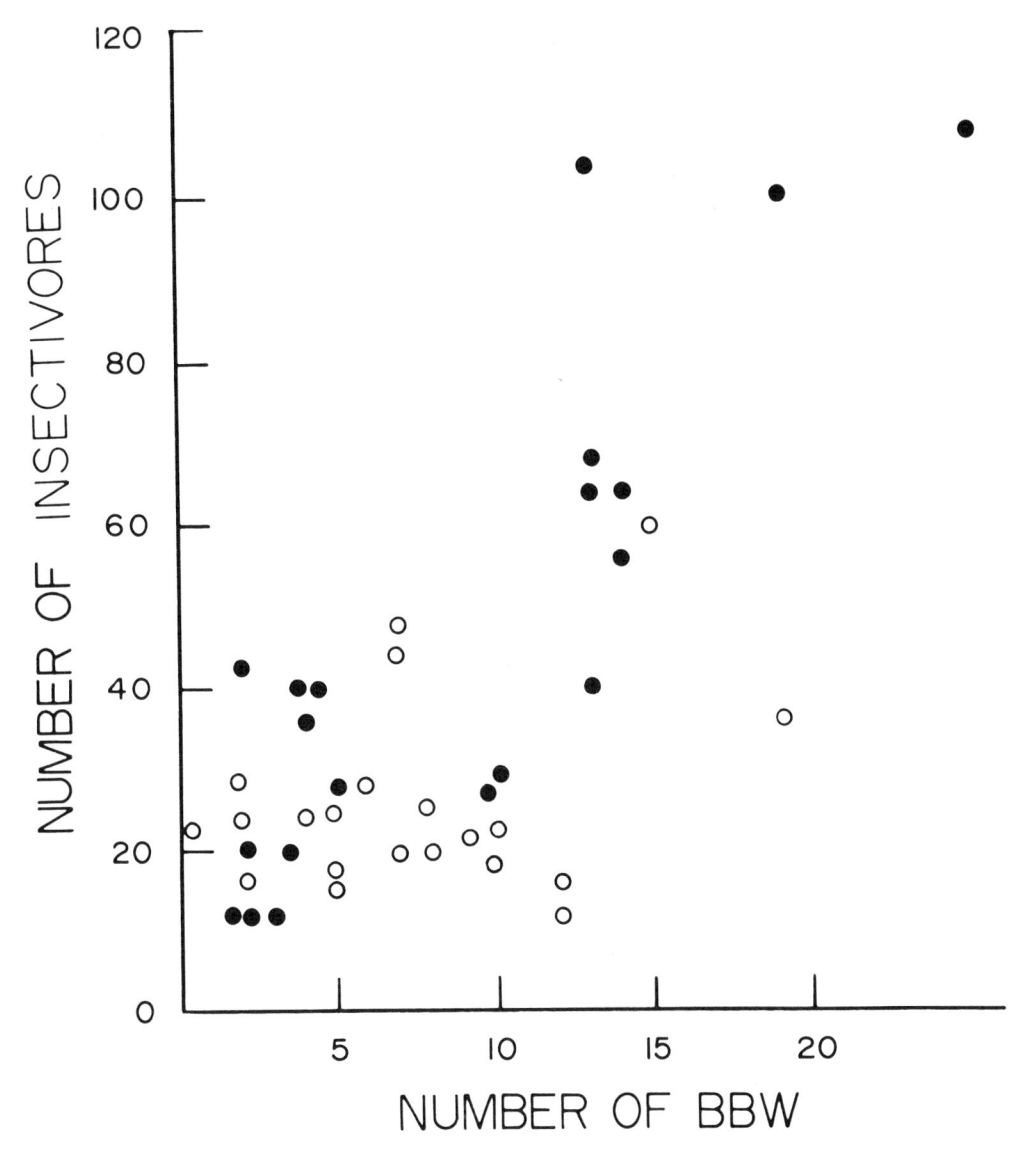

FIG. 7. Scatter plot of total number of Bay-breasted Warbler versus the number of resident insectivorous bird sightings for each transect unit during each winter for the Wheeler and Snyder-Molino transects. Data from the Wheeler transect are indicated by closed circles ($Y = 3.9 X + 9.9$, $r = 0.83$); Snyder-Molino data are indicated by open circles ($Y = 0.84 X + 20.1$, $r = 0.30$).

GROUP SIZE IN BAY-BREASTED AND CHESTNUT-SIDED WARBLERS

BAY-BREASTED WARBLER

Bay-breasted Warblers occur both solitarily and in groups. In the Canal Area most were found in small groups. Group size distribution for BCI was consistent from year to year, with approximately one-third of all Bay-breasted Warblers occurring solitarily and an average group size of about three for nonsolitary birds (range = 2-12). The distribution of group sizes on BCI was similar to that of other habitats and localities in the Canal Area (Table 5). The combined data from off- and on-island sites are statistically indistinguishable.

I recorded considerably larger group sizes during my three trips to the Pirre region of Darien (Table 5). Groups averaged 5-9, with a number of sightings of groups of between 10 and 20 individuals. These large flocks were found both in the canopy of mature forests and in the young second growth along the Rio Pirre.

The nature of these groups of Bay-breasted Warblers is unclear. Groups were generally loose and the movement of individuals slow; the degree to which Bay-breasted Warblers follow each other, forming cohesive flocks, is difficult to discern. The situation may be similar to the flocks of Yellow-rumped Warblers (*Dendroica coronata*), which also tend to be loose in structure and slow in their progression (Morse 1970; Rappole and Warner 1980; Greenberg ms). Yellow-rumped Warblers, however, often bolt, flying long distances to a new habitat patch; during these flights, group cohesion is often maintained. I observed no such behavior in the Bay-breasted Warbler; nor did they forage in tight groups that moved from tree to tree such as is characteristic of Tennessee Warblers (Skutch 1957; Morton 1980; Tramer and Kemp 1980; pers. obs.). Apparent sociality in Bay-breasted Warblers may be no more than different individuals aggregating at the same location. This location may be attractive because of a rich food resource, such as a fruiting tree, or the presence of a mixed species flock. The major social antecedent of this level of sociality would be the absence of territorial defense.

One line of evidence that suggests that groups may form as a result of individuals independently joining mixed species flocks is that group size is considerably larger for birds in mixed flocks than out of mixed flocks (Table 6). If Bay-breasted Warblers characteristically travel in single species flocks, then observations of these flocks out of mixed species associations should be relatively common; in fact, they are very rare. While this observation suggests that Bay-breasted Warblers are aggregating at mixed species flocks, another possible mechanism for this pattern is that Bay-breasted Warbler flocks are joined by other

Table 5. Group size of Bay-breasted Warbler on BCI and in other parts of Panama: percentage of total individuals in different group sizes (fruiting aggregations not included)

Group Size	BCI 1976 n = 150	BCI 1977-78 n = 367	BCI 1978-79 n = 549	Canal Zone 1976-79 n = 212	Darien 1978-79 n = 427
1	35	35	37	33	21
2	22	22	21	24	7
3	20	20	24	17	9
4	15	9	12	19	8
5	5	6	5	5	4
6	2	2	2	3	3
7	1	0	0	0	11
8	0	1	0	0	0
9	0	0	0	0	0
10	0	0	0	0	0
11+	2	0	0	0	35
% individuals in groups (> 1)	65	65	63	67	78
$\bar{X}$ flock size	2.8	3.4	2.8	2.8	5.0

Table 6. Group size distribution for Bay-breasted Warblers in and out of mixed-species flocks on BCI: percentage of individuals in each group size

Group Size	In MSF (n = 609)	Out of MSF (n = 210)
1	25	66
2	27	15
3	24	14
4	12	0
5	6	5
6	2	0
7+	4	0

x^2 = 133.2, d.f. = 4, p < .001

species as nuclei for mixed-species flock formation. The small loose groups characteristic of the Canal Area seem to be unlikely candidates for nuclei of mixed-species flocks (Moynihan 1962; Willis 1972), particularly when the noisy and conspicuous family groups of *Hylophilus*, *Microrhopias*, and certain tanagers occur in the same mixed flocks. In Darien, however, we observed mixed flocks that consisted only of large groups of Bay-breasted Warblers and solitary attendant species such as *Rhynchocyclus olivaceus*, *Xenerpestes minlosi*, *Xiphorynchus*, etc. I observed four of these flocks over several hour intervals, and the array of solitary attendant species changed, as the Bay-breasted Warbler flock moved through the second growth. Perhaps the mere size of the Darien Bay-breasted Warbler flocks makes them attractive to wandering solitary residents.

The distribution of the number of Bay-breasted Warblers per mixed species flock on BCI deviates slightly, but significantly from a Poisson distribution (Table 7). Poisson distribution is the expected distribution of group size if warblers join mixed species flocks independently of each other. The additional assumption, however, is that all mixed species flocks are equally attractive to warblers. This is most certainly not true; flocks that have any Bay-breasted Warblers tend to have more resident species ($\bar{X} = 6$) than flocks without warblers [($\bar{X} = 5$) (U = 20667, p < .001)]. The slightly clumped distribution of Bay-breasted Warblers at mixed species flocks could result from a tendency of small groups of warblers to join mixed flocks or from particular mixed-species flocks attracting more solitary warblers.

The existence of long-term foci of activity also argues against Bay-breasted Warbler groups being coherent single-species flocks. Groups of Bay-breasted

Table 7. Number of Bay-breasted Warblers in mixed-species flocks compared with an expected Poisson distribution

Number	1978 (n = 302) Observed	Expected	1979 (n = 259) Observed	Expected
0	54	46	42	35
1	29	36	31	37
2	9	13.5	13	19
3	7	3	9	6.5
4	1	0.5	2	2
5	0.3	0	2	0.3
6	0	0	0.3	0.001
χ^2	23.15, d.f. = 4, p < .001		13.92, d.f. = 5, p < .001	

Warblers may be found consistently in the same locality in the forest through and between winters. One such group could be observed from the BCI canopy tower. The warblers in this group followed mixed flocks as they passed through the area, but remained behind when the flock moved on. The occurrence of groups of Bay-breasted Warblers results in part from the shared habitat preference of the warblers and the species that form mixed species flocks. This suggestion is supported by the correlation between overall bird density and Bay-breasted Warbler density on census transects.

In summary, on BCI it is possible that little true intraspecific flocking occurs in Bay-breasted Warblers; groups form by aggregation at fruiting trees, local habitat patches, or mixed species flocks. The cohesive single species flocks of Bay-breasted Warblers in Darien are similar to those formed by Tennessee Warblers in other parts of Central America (Skutch 1957; Morton 1980; pers. obs.).

CHESTNUT-SIDED WARBLER

Chestnut-sided Warblers show no such tendencies to aggregate or flock. My observations on BCI and off-island sites for three winters (Table 8) are consistent; Chestnut-sided Warblers occur alone. A small proportion of individuals occur in twos, and once I observed three individuals together. Since I have become familiar with the rapid and subtle sequence of territorial boundary displays, I would now interpret all instances of co-occurrence that I observed as involving territorial skirmishes. Morton (1980) suggested that Chestnut-sided Warblers, while not as "socially tolerant" as Bay-breasted Warblers, do occur in groups. The size and frequency of these groups was not discussed, nor was the possibility of territorial interaction excluded.

If aggregation is an important mechanism of group formation in warblers, then density should be an important determinant of group size. Density will affect the number of individuals available to join mixed species flocks or that occur at a good

Table 8. Group size of Chestnut-sided Warbler on BCI and other localities: percentage of individuals in different group sizes

Group Size	BCI 1976 (n=80)	BCI 1977-78 (n=136)	BCI 1978-79 (n=133)	Canal Zone 1976-79 (n=58)	La Selva 1978 (n=69)
1	90	96	97	90	94
2[a]	10	4	3	4	6
3	0	0	0	6	0

a. Includes birds in territorial disputes.

habitat patch. The lack of groups of Chestnut-sided Warblers may be a trivial consequence of lower density. Several lines of evidence, however, suggest that this is not the case:

The distribution of Chestnut-sided Warblers per mixed species flock (Table 9) is truncated and significantly different from a Poisson distribution. In other words, given the number of Chestnut-sided Warblers observed in flocks, more flocks with two or more Chestnut-sided Warblers should have been observed if these warblers were joining flocks independently.

When two Chestnut-sided Warblers were observed in the same flock they were invariably involved in territorial interactions.

Where Chestnut-sided Warblers are extremely common (e.g., Costa Rica) they still appear to be largely solitary. This is in sharp contrast to Bay-breasted Warblers which occur in larger flocks at higher density.

The evidence for this last point comes primarily from the survey I conducted at La Selva, where, based on the number of Chestnut-sided Warblers observed per hour of field work, I estimated Chestnut-sided Warblers to be five times more numerous than in the Canal Area; in four days I found 3.0/hr as opposed to 0.5-1.0/hr in the Canal Area. In this situation, the same proportion of twosomes were observed (Table 8), and the non-solitary birds were involved in territorial skirmishes. Skutch (1957) and Slud (1964) reported that Chestnut-sided Warblers were generally solitary in Costa Rica.

It should be apparent that the exploitation systems of the two warblers, as indicated by group size, have not diverged in sympatry, nor is the difference in flocking behavior a unique feature to Canal Area populations. The difference in single species sociality between the two species has been noted during migration in the eastern United States as well (Manolis pers. comm.).

Table 9. Distribution of the number of Chestnut-sided Warblers in mixed-species flocks on BCI compared to an expected Poisson distribution

Number	Observed (n = 561)	Expected	Chi-square[a]
0	60	67	3.5
1	39	27	28.8
2	1	5	18.9

a. Total χ^2 = 55.2, d.f. = 3, p < .0001

MIXED-SPECIES FLOCKING

Both Bay-breasted and Chestnut-sided warblers are usually found in mixed-species flocks on BCI. Bay-breasted Warblers were found significantly less often in mixed flocks than Chestnut-sided Warblers (Table 10). In all seasons, except early 1977-1978, 79% of the Bay-breasted Warblers, as opposed to 90-95% of the Chestnut-sided Warblers, were in mixed flocks. The low value (56%) for early 1977-1978 for the Bay-breasted Warbler included data gathered in October, when warbler densities were higher and more transients were present.

Most mixed species flocks on Barro Colorado Island (BCI) during the winter months have one of the species of *Dendroica* (62-69%); over half (57-59%) had Bay-breasted and 40% had Chestnut-sided warblers. The two species tend to co-occur in mixed flocks more than is expected by random association (Table 10), with 26-28% of the flocks containing both species. In fact, approximately 70% of the flocks with Chestnut-sided also had Bay-breasted Warblers; whereas, half the flocks with Bay-breasted Warblers also had Chestnut-sided Warblers.

The most common associates of warblers include antwrens, woodcreepers, hover-gleaning flycatchers, and tanagers. Warblers occur in a subset of mixed flocks that has a significantly different composition from all mixed flocks observed (Table 11). Considering the 13 most common species (> .10 frequency), five species occurred in a disproportionately greater frequency in flocks that had either Chestnut-sided or Bay-breasted warblers (based on X^2 test of association p < .05). These include species that are characteristic of the upper strata of the BCI forest, *Hylophilus decurtatus*, *Tachyphonus*, *Tolmomyias*, *Polioptila plumbea* and *Dacnis cayana*. Flocks with either species of warblers tended to have fewer *Myrmotherula* antwrens and *Thamnophilus* than expected.

Bay-breasted and Chestnut-sided warblers associate differently with the common flocking species. The Bay-breasted Warbler is strongly associated with *Hylophilus decurtatus*, *Tachyphonus luctuosus*, *Tolmomyias assimilis*, and *Polioptila plumbea* and is significantly negatively associated with the antbirds, *Myrmotherula fulviventris*, *M. axillaris*, and *Thamnophilus punctatus* (Table 12). The Chestnut-sided Warbler was less strongly associated with the canopy species and was not negatively associated with the understory antbirds (Table 13).

I examined the composition of flocks that had either Chestnut-sided or Bay-breasted warblers, but not both species, to determine the differences in flock associates of the two species (Table 14). My reasoning is that the flocks where

Table 10. Participation in mixed-species flocks by Bay-breasted and Chestnut-sided warblers on BCI (all figures are percentages)

	1978 302 flocks	1979 259 flocks
Flocks with either species	62	69
Flocks with Bay-breasted Warbler	47	59
Flocks with Chestnut-sided Warbler	41	38
Flocks with both species[a]	26	28
Flocks with Chestnut-sided Warblers that also have Bay-breasted Warblers	64	72
Flocks with Bay-breasted Warblers that also have Chestnut-sided Warblers	56	47
Percentage of Bay-breasted Warblers in mixed-species flocks		
early winter	56 (223)[b]	79 (379)
late winter	80 (144)	79 (226)
Total	65 (367)	79 (521)
Percentage of Chestnut-sided Warblers in mixed species flocks		
early winter	90 (60)	95 (64)
late winter	90 (74)	91 (87)
Total	90 (134)	93 (171)

a. X^2 values of association between the two species are 24.4 ($p < .01$) for 1978 and 12.8 ($p < .01$) for 1979.
b. Number of warbler sightings.

Table 11. Frequency of common flocking species in mixed-species flocks with *Dendroica* compared to flocks without *Dendroica* (296 with and 172 without *Dendroica*)

Species	Frequency in warbler flocks	Freq. warbler/ Freq. no warbler[a]	Association[b]
Myrmotherula fulviventris	.54	.78	− 10.2
M. axillaris	.33	.70	− 9.2
Microrhopias quixensis	.66	.91	=
Hylophylax naevioides	.10	.63	=
Thamnophilus punctatus	.34	.72	− 27.2
Xenops minutus	.19	1.1	=
Glyphorynchus spirurus	.14	1.3	=
Tolmomyias assimilis	.19	4.8	+ 27.2
Terenotriccus erythrurus	.13	.85	=
Polioptila plumbea	.11	5.5	+ 10.7
Hylophilus decurtatus	.55	2.6	+ 50.7
Dacnis cayana	.14	2.3	+ 7.9
Tachyphonus luctuosus	.33	2.5	+ 23.7

a. The ratio of the frequency of the species in mixed flocks with Bay-breasted or Chestnut-sided warblers and those without warblers.
b. Sign indicates whether the association was negative, positive, or if no association was discernable. x^2 values are presented for significant associations.

Table 12. Frequency of common flocking species in mixed-species flocks with Bay-breasted Warblers compared to flocks without Bay-breasted Warblers (239 with and 229 without, see Table 11)

Species	Frequency in BBW flocks	Freq. BBW/ Freq. no BBW	Association
Myrmotherula fulviventris	.52	.76	− 6.7
M. axillaris	.33	.73	− 6.1
Microrhopias quixensis	.64	1.0	=
Hylophylax naevioides	.10	.67	=
Thamnophilus punctatus	.33	.75	− 6.2
Xenops minutus	.20	1.2	=
Glyphorynchus spirurus	.14	1.2	=
Tolmomyias assimilis	.22	4.2	=
Terenotriccus erythrurus	.13	.85	=
Hylophilus decurtatus	.40	2.1	+ 24.5
Polioptila plumbea	.12	4.0	+ 13.0
Dacnis cayana	.13	2.6	+ 8.5
Tachyphonus luctuosus	.36	2.6	+ 29.5

Table 13. Frequency of common flocking species in mixed-species flocks with Chestnut-sided Warblers compared with flocks without Chestnut-sided Warblers (170 with and 298 without, see Table 11)

Species	Frequency in CSW flocks	Freq. CSW/ Freq. no CSW	Association
Myrmotherula fulviventris	.58	.95	=
M. axillaris	.35	.88	=
Microrhopias quixensis	.71	1.2	+ 5.2
Hylophylax naevioides	.11	.84	=
Thamnophilus punctatus	.32	.76	=
Xenops minutus	.18	1.0	=
Glyphorynchus spirurus	.18	1.8	+ 4.3
Xiphorhynchus lachrymosus	.13	1.4	=
Tolmomyias assimilis	.19	1.9	+ 7.6
Hylophilus decurtatus	.58	1.6	+ 4.2
Dacnis cayana	.14	2.0	+ 10.2
Tachyphonus luctuosus	.36	1.6	+ 16.6

Table 14. Frequency of occurrence of common flocking species in mixed-species flocks with Chestnut-sided Warblers (no Bay-breasted Warblers) and Bay-breasted Warblers (no Chestnut-sided Warblers, n = 57, 126, respectively)

Species	Frequency in CSW flock	Frequency in BBW flock	Chi-square[a]
Myrmotherula fulviventris	.63	.50	
M. axillaris	.35	.31	
Microrhopias quixensis	.77	.61	4.13
Hylophylax naevioides	.10	.09	
Thamnophilus punctatus	.35	.36	
Xenops minutus	.14	.19	
Glyphorynchus spirurus	.12	.08	
Terenotriccus erythrurus	.12	.10	
Polioptila plumbea	.05	.12	
Hylophilus decurtatus	.43	.55	
Dacnis cayana	.07	.10	
Tachyphonus luctuosus	.19	.33	

a. Chi-square value given for significant differences.

both species occur should provide no information on the differences in interspecific associates of the two species. Chestnut-sided Warblers were found with significantly greater frequency with *Microrhopias*; whereas, Bay-breasted Warblers were found more frequently (but not quite significantly) with *Tolmomyias assimilis*, *Tachyphonus luctuosus*, and *Polioptia plumbea*.

Warblers do not join individual species, but rather groups of species that themselves tend to co-occur. Willis (1972) suggested that such groups occur among the forest flocks on BCI; he described an understory "alliance" centered around *Myrmotherula axillaris* and a canopy alliance associated with *Hylophilus decurtatus*. Jones (1977), however, found few significant associations between species occurring in mixed species flocks on BCI. Indeed, many flocks have large height ranges and are populated with both canopy and understory species, thus obscuring any tendency towards stratification of smaller flocks. I attempted to assess whether, within this variability, alliances can be discerned on the basis of coefficients of association. The analysis is based on the 486 flock censuses in the mixed species flocking survey.

I ran the necessary 105 tests of association for the pair-wise association of the 15 most common species (Table 15). I used the following simple algorithm to define the clusters of significantly associated species: (1) Form the largest set of species that are totally interconnected by significant associations; (2) For remaining species determine the scores of associations with the species in the

Table 15. Significant association between members of mixed-species flocks based on chi-square tests of association: + indicates a significant positive association (p < .05), − indicates a significant negative association, and 0 indicates no association.

	MF	Ma	Hn	Tp	Mg	Xm	Te	Gs	Ta	Pp	Hd	Dc	Tl	BBW	CSW
Myrmotherula fulviventris															
M. axillaris	+														
Hylophylax naevioides	+	+													
Thamnophilus punctatus	+	+	+												
Microrhopias quixensis	+	+	0	0											
Xenops minutus	0	+	+	0	0										
Terenotriccus erythrurus	0	0	+	0	0	0									
Glyphorynchus spirurus	0	+	0	0	0	0	0								
Tolmomyias assimilis	0	0	0	0	0	0	0	0							
Polioptila plumbea	−	0	0	0	0	+	0	0	+						
Hylophilus decurtatus	−	0	0	0	0	+	0	+	+	+					
Dacnis cayana	−	0	0	0	0	0	0	0	+	+	+				
Tachyphonus luctuosus	−	0	0	0	−	+	0	+	+	+	+	+			
Bay-breasted Warbler	−	−	0	−	−	0	0	0	+	+	+	+	+		
Chestnut-sided Warbler	0	0	0	0	0	0	0	0	+	+	+	+	+	+	

already formed cluster. These scores are computed as follows: (positive associations-negative association) ÷ number of comparisons. (3) Add the species with the highest association score to the appropriate cluster; these new clusters will be used with remaining species in step 1.

The associations formed by this method are depicted in Figure 8. The two initial clusters include two species of antwrens, *Hylophylax*, and *Thamnophilus*, and a set of canopy species. *Xenops* and *Microrhopias* show associations with both canopy and antwren flock species, but more with the latter species. *Glyphorynchus* is loosely associated with canopy species. Members of the canopy flock alliance show a large number of significant negative associations (11/49 comparisons) with antwren alliance members. Both Bay-breasted and Chestnut-sided warblers were solid members of the canopy alliance; the Chestnut-sided Warbler, however, showed no negative associations with any of the antwren alliance species and was positively associated with *Microrhopias*.

In Darien, Bay-breasted Warblers were found in association with a similar array of species as found in the Canal Area. Only a few were seen in antwren flocks, however, as warblers were scarce in forest understory. Most Bay-breasted Warblers were observed in young second-growth or the outer canopy of mature forest, and were associated with small omnivorous birds characteristic of these habitats. Bay-breasted Warblers were observed particularly frequently with *Tolmomyias*, *Hylophilus decurtatus*, and *Hemithraupis* (Table 16).

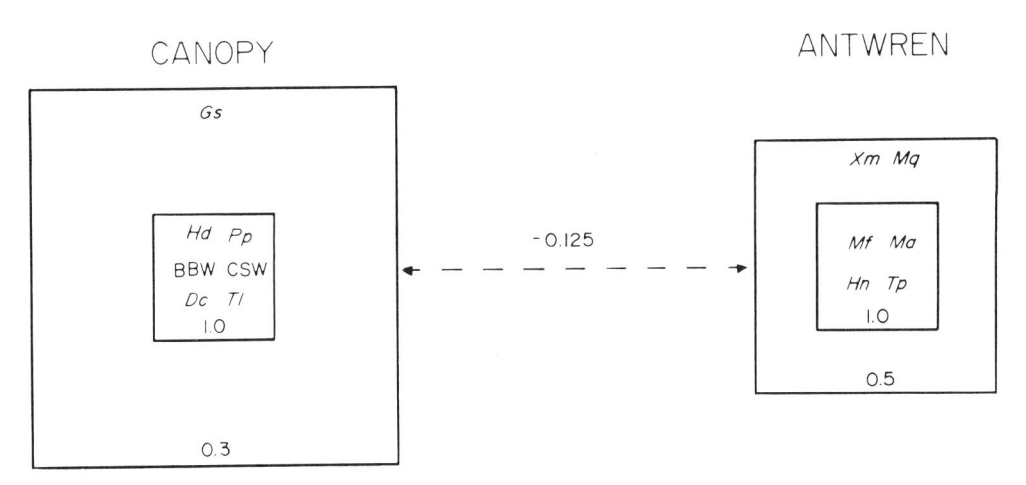

FIG. 8. "Alliances" of species that tend to co-occur in mixed species flocks more than expected by random association. Lines surround clusters with the indicated association score (see p. 40). See Table 15 for abbreviations.

Table 16. Common flocking associates of Bay-breasted Warblers in the Pirre Region, December and February 1978 and February 1979 (53 flocks)

Species or species groups	Frequency[a]
Tolmomyias assimilis	.41
Hemithraupis flavicollis	.15
Hylophilus decurtatus	.15
Tangara inornata	.13
Xenops minutus	.13
Tangara larvata	.11
Capito maculicoronatus	.11
Tachyphonus luctuosus	.10
Piranga rubra	.07
Cyanerpes lucidus	.07
Automalus ochrolaemus	.07
Conirostrum leucogenys	.06
Microrhopias quixensis	.06
Rhynchocylcus olivaceus	.06
Tityra inquisitor	.05
Venilornis kirkii	.05
Dendrocinclidae species	.22
Euphonia sp.	.20
Polioptila sp.	.15
Icterus sp.	.07
Pachyramphus sp.	.09

a. Frequency in mixed species flocks that have at least one Bay-breasted Warbler.

CLOSE ASSOCIATES OF WARBLERS

The work of Moynihan (1962) on honeycreeper-tanager flocks in lowland clearings and bush tanager flocks in the highlands of Panama emphasized the importance of within-flock associations between species. Moynihan described flock "roles" based on the following and leading responses of members of mixed flocks. Information of this sort, while potentially useful in describing interspecific relations, is difficult to obtain for tropical forest flocks. Members of the flock tend to be widely dispersed and meander slowly through the uninterrupted vegetation, rather than bolting from tree to tree as do tanager flocks. While certain species, notably antwrens, tend to initiate movement in a certain direction and other species (woodcreepers, flycatchers, warblers, etc.) tend to follow, general flock movement always appears diffuse. To obtain quantitative information of where warblers occur in the spatial array of a mixed flock, I recorded the species present within five m of warblers I selected for detailed foraging observations. This spherical volume around the warbler will be referred to as its "neighborhood." While this may not measure the behavioral interactions in the manner of Moynihan or Morse (1970), it at least defines the immediate social environment of a warbler.

The number of species in the neighborhood of a foraging warbler reflects both the propensity of warblers to join flocks and the tendency of flock joining warblers to forage near resident birds. It is not surprising that Bay-breasted Warblers foraged near only half the number of other species, on the average, than did Chestnut-sided Warblers (0.36 versus 0.78, $X^2 = 29.3$, d.f. = 3, $p < .001$, based on proportion of warblers with 0, 1, 2, or 3 or more species within 5 m). Differences between the warblers persist even when only warblers in mixed species flocks are considered; Bay-breasted Warblers still have fewer neighbors (0.45 versus 0.78, $X^2 = 21.5$, d.f. = 3, $p < .001$). Chestnut-sided Warblers have a high frequency of *Microrhopias* in their neighborhood (Table 17); roughly one-quarter of all Chestnut-sided Warblers have a pair of or an individual antwren within 5 m. The mean distance between Chestnut-sided Warblers and the nearest *Microrhopias* (in the same flock) was estimated to be 10 m (S.D. = 8 m), based on 50 observations. The neighborhood of the Chestnut-sided Warbler was dominated by *Hylophilus*, *Thamnophilus*, and *Myrmotherula fulviventris*; whereas, that of the Bay-breasted Warbler, exhibited more equatable numbers of *Microrhopias*, *Myrmotherula fulviventris*, *Hylophilus*, *Thamnophilus*, and *Tachyphonus*.

Table 17. Close associates of Bay-breasted and Chestnut-sided Warblers on BCI (see Table 15 for abbreviations)

Bay Breasted	Mq	Mf	Ma	Tp	Hd	Tl	Dc	CSW
Neighborhood frequency[a] (n = 196 flocks)	.10	.07	.01	.05	.08	.05	.01	.13
Frequency of co-occurrence in the same flock	.64	.52	.34	.34	.57	.36	.13	.52
Close Association frequency[b]	.16	.13	.03	.18	.14	.14	.08	.23

Chestnut-sided	Mq	Mf	Ma	Tp	Hd	Tl	Dc	BBW
Neighborhood frequency (n = 191 flocks)	.26	.12	.04	.05	.12	.05	.01	.17
Frequency of co-occurrence in the same flock	.72	.58	.35	.33	.55	.34	.14	.70
Close Association frequency	.36	.21	.11	.15	.22	.07	.07	.24

a. Frequency of occurrence within 5 m of a warbler.
b. Frequency of occurrence within 5 m of a warbler divided by the frequency of co-occurrence in the same mixed-species flock.

The close associations result from both the tendency of warblers to co-occur with these species in the same flock and their propensity to forage in proximity within the same flock. To further examine the tendency of warblers to forage near other species (given that they are in the same flock), I divided the frequency of a species occurrence within the neighborhood of the warbler by the frequency of co-occurrence in the same flocks. I will refer to the standardized values as close association values. The Bay-breasted Warbler shows high values for *Micorhopias*, *Myrmotherula fulviventris*, *Thamnophilus*, *Hylophilus*, and *Tachyphonus* (Table 17). The Chestnut-sided Warbler has high values for *Microrhopias*, *Myrmotherula fulviventris* and *Thamnophilus* and low values for *Myrmotherula axillaris*, *Dacnis*, and *Tachyphonus*.

Similarity in foraging height distributions should be an important factor in determining the tendency of species to associate closely within flocks. The

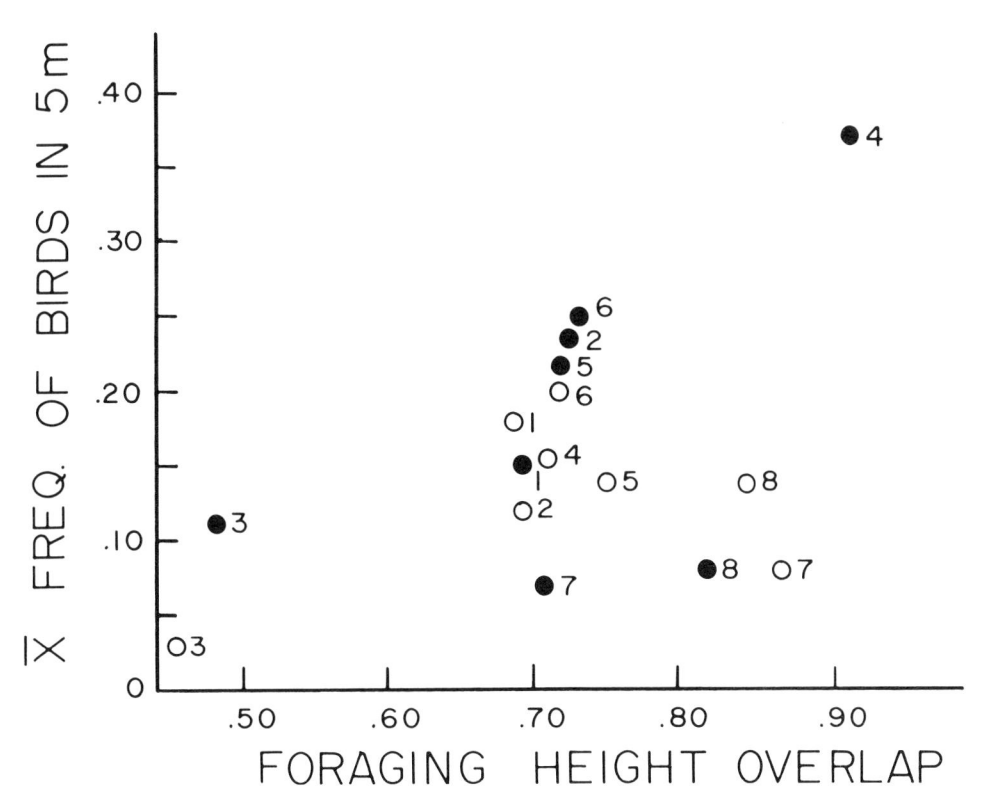

FIG. 9. Scatter diagram of Close Association index values versus the foraging height overlap between some common flocking species and Bay-breasted (open circles) and Chestnut-sided (closed circles) warblers. Close association values consist of the frequency of occurrence within five meters of a warbler divided by the frequency of co-occurrence in the same mixed species flocks as warblers. Species codes are as follows: 1 = *Thamnophilus punctatus*, 2 = *Myrmotherula fulviventris*, 3 = *M. axillaris*, 4 = *Microrhopias quixensis*, 5 = *Hylophilus decurtatus*, 6 = Bay-breasted or Chestnut-sided warbler, 7 = *Dacnis cayana*, and 8 = *Tachyphonus luctuosus*.

neighborhood is, after all, a sphere that extends both horizontally and vertically. Foraging height overlap values (see Foraging Behavior) poorly predict the degree of within flock association (Fig. 9) (r_s for both species pooled = 0.7, d.f. = 16, n.s.; r_s for CSW only = .68, d.f. = 8, $p < .05$, r_s BBW = .23). The 0.36 value for the association between *Microrhopias* and the Chestnut-sided Warbler, for example, is a distant outlier from the mass of uncorrelated values of 0.65-0.90 height overlaps versus 0.03-0.22 close associations.

This high close association value between the Chestnut-sided Warbler and *Micorhopias* supports my subjective impression that Chestnut-sided Warblers track the movements of the *Microrhopias* family group when moving in a mixed flock. Still, the distance between the warbler and the antwrens is usually great in terms of the possibility of visual contact. Ten meters in a tropical forest usually contains some profound obstruction, which would be exacerbated in this case since *Microrhopias* forages in very dense vegetation (Wiley 1971). On the other hand, *Microrhopias* is the noisiest of the antwrens; the loud whistled contact calls should be easily located. For an intensive forager like the Chestnut-sided Warbler, *Microrhopias* is probably the easiest species to follow in order to keep track of flock movements in dense vegetation.

SUPPLANTATIONS AND CHASES

Supplantations and short chases comprise the bulk of the observations of interspecific aggression among forest passerines (Morse 1970). The relative number and direction of interactions are probably the best indicators of possible dominance relationships between individuals of different species. I recorded all instances of aggressive acts that I observed during the three winters (Table 18).

Aggressive interactions were rarely observed, particularly between insectivorous residents and migrants. During the three field seasons, I observed only two interactions involving antwrens and warblers. In one case, a *Microrhopias* briefly chased a Magnolia Warbler and in the second case *Myrmotherula fulviventris* chased a Chestnut-sided Warbler. In fact, interspecific aggression among migrants occurred much more frequently than migrant-resident interactions. Bay-breasted Warblers, for example, were involved in 29 observed interactions with other migrants and in only 21 with residents. For the Chestnut-sided Warbler, the ratio of interactions with migrants to interactions with residents was 21:4. Indeed, intraspecific interactions among migrants, particularly for Bay-breasted and Tennessee Warblers, were the most commonly observed aggressive acts.

Residents nearly always supplanted or chased migrants rather than being supplanted or chased. Most instances of residents chasing warblers involved omnivorous species (21:4). In these cases even small resident species (*Pipromorpha oleaginea*, *Tyranniscus vilissimus*, *Hylophilus*) were observed to displace larger warblers. *Myiarchus tuberculifer* consistently harassed warblers that came to feed on *Miconia argentea* berries. Among the warblers, Bay-breasted Warblers were generally dominant to the smaller Chestnut-sided and Tennessee warblers (20 chases:2 chased). Interactions with Magnolia Warblers were too few to evaluate.

Table 18. The number of chases and supplantations between warblers and other birds on BCI

	BBW	CSW	TW	All Migrants	Total	Residents Omnivore	Insectivore
Bay-breasted Warbler	30	14:2[a]	6:2	25:4	4:17	4:14	0:3
Chestnut-sided Warbler	2:14	--[b]	1:0	5:15	0:4	0:3	0:1

a. Aggressors given first; in this case, Bay-breasted Warblers chased or supplanted Chestnut-sided Warblers 14 times and were chased 2 times.
b. Territorial interactions not included.

SPACING BEHAVIOR

BAY-BREASTED WARBLER

The Bay-breasted Warbler has a largely overlapping spacing system on Barro Colorado Island (BCI). Individuals have large overlapping home-ranges. Four observations suggest this is true:

> Bay-breasted Warblers are gregarious and do not show the truncated distribution of individuals per mixed species flock that is characteristic of Chestnut-sided and Canada warblers (above, p. 34; Greenberg and Gradwohl 1980a).
> Resightings of small numbers of marked birds are consistent with the hypothesized overlapping home-range system. These observations will be discussed in detail below.
> High densities of warblers at particular fruiting trees indicate that they aggregated from a large area. These aggregations are often three to six times larger than the average flock size, so they should not form unless the fruiting trees are within or near the foraging range of individual warblers (Greenberg 1981a).
> I observed few aggressive interactions among Bay-breasted Warblers other than supplantations from particular branches. I observed only four individuals that appeared to be defending an area by chasing other warblers away. These occurred at local rich food sources such as a flowering or fruiting tree (Greenberg 1981a) or insects on a screen near an insect light.

Bay-breasted Warblers are difficult to mist-net because they generally forage at great heights in the forest. During certain periods, they forage low in light gap vegetation and near the ground in the BCI laboratory clearing; a few individuals were captured. Despite the small sample size, a consistent picture emerged from the resightings of these marked Bay-breasted Warblers. Individuals were occasionally localized for short periods, but in general they were observed only sporadically. Often an individual would disappear for up to three months (Fig. 10) The two areas where Bay-breasted Warblers were marked were patrolled nearly daily by J. Gradwohl and myself searching specifically for color-marked birds.

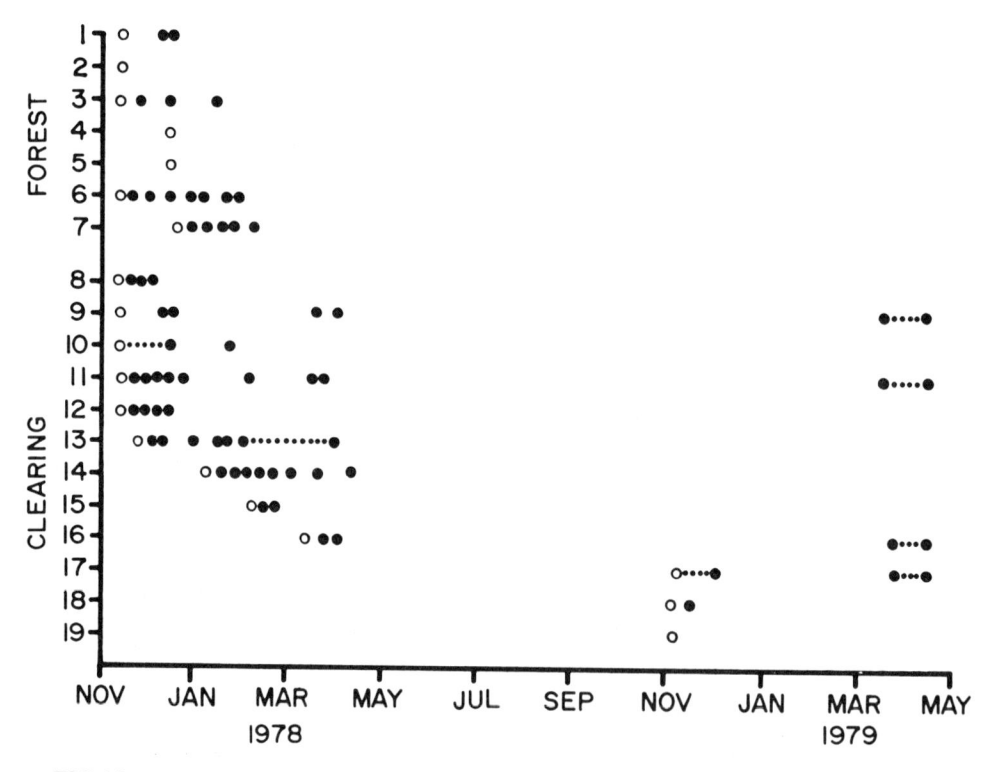

FIG.10. The temporal pattern of resightings of marked or recognizable Bay-breasted Warblers on BCI. Open circles denote the date of first sighting or capture; dotted lines cover periods of daily sightings.

Between resightings of double-orange, for example, I made 55 resightings of unmarked Bay-breasted Warblers on the 6 ha plateau study site. Clearing birds showed up at a particular fruiting tree after a resighting gap of three months (5 in 1977-1978 and 4 in 1978-1979); for two individuals the hiatus was a year. I continually patrolled the clearing so these birds were certainly absent from the area during the gaps. For birds that showed some localization, no area of exclusive use could be discerned. One marked bird did attempt to defend a fruiting *Miconia argentea* for at least 10 days. A few of the clearing birds were resighted frequently and most were sighted rarely. This pattern of resighting is also found in *Glyphorynchus spirurus* and *Pipra mentalis* on BCI (Gradwohl and Greenberg unpubl. data) and suggests that the home-ranges consist of a heavily used core area in the center of a large home-range.

CHESTNUT-SIDED WARBLER

The Chestnut-sided Warbler has a rigid territorial system on BCI. This assertion is supported with data from the monitoring of individually recognizable birds through two winters; the observation of high levels of aggression at consistent boundary areas; and the highly vocal response of Chestnut-sided Warblers to play-backs of conspecific call notes.

Resighting of individuals in the BCI clearing indicates largely exclusive home-ranges are maintained by all individuals. The overlap that was observed occurred when the individual associated with the intruded territory was not in the area. Usually (six out of eight times) the trespassing act was followed within five minutes by a long-distance chase as the resident individual returned. Individuals preceded trespassing by perching conspicuously and chipping loudly for several minutes. During October 1978, three warblers were observed or marked and not located again; after this, the territorial array in the BCI clearing was stable and all individuals survived the winter.

Territoriality based on the criterion of overt aggression was harder to discern among Chestnut-sided Warblers in the forest. The most formidable evidence is the observation of highly exclusive home ranges maintained throughout both winters (Fig. 11). Loud chipping, so prevalent among clearing warblers, was practically unheard in the forest. Border displays are so obscure that I did not observe any until the winter of 1978-1979. Two factors probably account for the increased subtlety of territorial maintenance behavior. First, territories are larger and vegetation denser. For the eight territories observed during the two winters in the forest, the mean size was approximately 1-1.5 ha. For five clearing territories, the average size was 0.2 ha. Second, the warblers were closely associated with antwren flocks (Gradwohl and Greenberg 1980) and all territorial interactions were restricted to occasions when antwren groups met at border interactions. The interaction between neighboring Chestnut-sided Warblers occurred rapidly and involved difficult to hear "zeet" notes (see below).

The distribution of territories in the BCI forest was identical to the array of *Myrmotherula fulviventris-Microrhopias* territories. Chestnut-sided Warblers essentially co-defend antwren territories. This accounts for the constancy of territorial boundaries between winters (Fig. 11), since antwren territories appear to be constant over many years (Greenberg and Gradwohl ms.). Chestnut-sided Warbler observations along trail systems are clustered (Fig. 12), which indicates a patchy distribution of territories, particularly in the old forest. The antwren groups with which Chestnut-sided Warblers so closely associate tend to use heavily local disturbances where vine-tangle densities are high (Gradwohl and Greenberg 1980). These areas are more patchily distributed in the old forest. Chestnut-sided Warbler territories in the forest showed little overlap, in contrast to the antwren territories with which they are associated. The warbler territories corresponded to the core defended area of antwren territories. As in the clearing birds, all territorial Chestnut-sided Warblers in the forest were observed throughout the winter, indicating high survivorship. The completely overlapping territories of antwrens and Chestnut-sided Warblers is similar to the multispecific territories of antwrens and other forest birds in Amazonian Forests (Munn and Terborgh 1979); the labile participation of a migrant species suggests that this spacing system is not necessarily highly co-evolved.

Territorial displays involve four distinct grades of aggression: chipping, fast chipping, zeeting, and long distance chasing. Warblers often give the aggressive vocalizations while puffing their body plumage and exposing any chestnut markings. I classified such markings as exposed, partially exposed, or unexposed every 10 seconds for birds that were foraging or giving territorial calls. Ninety percent of the territorial birds had exposed markings (N = 20), whereas only 20%

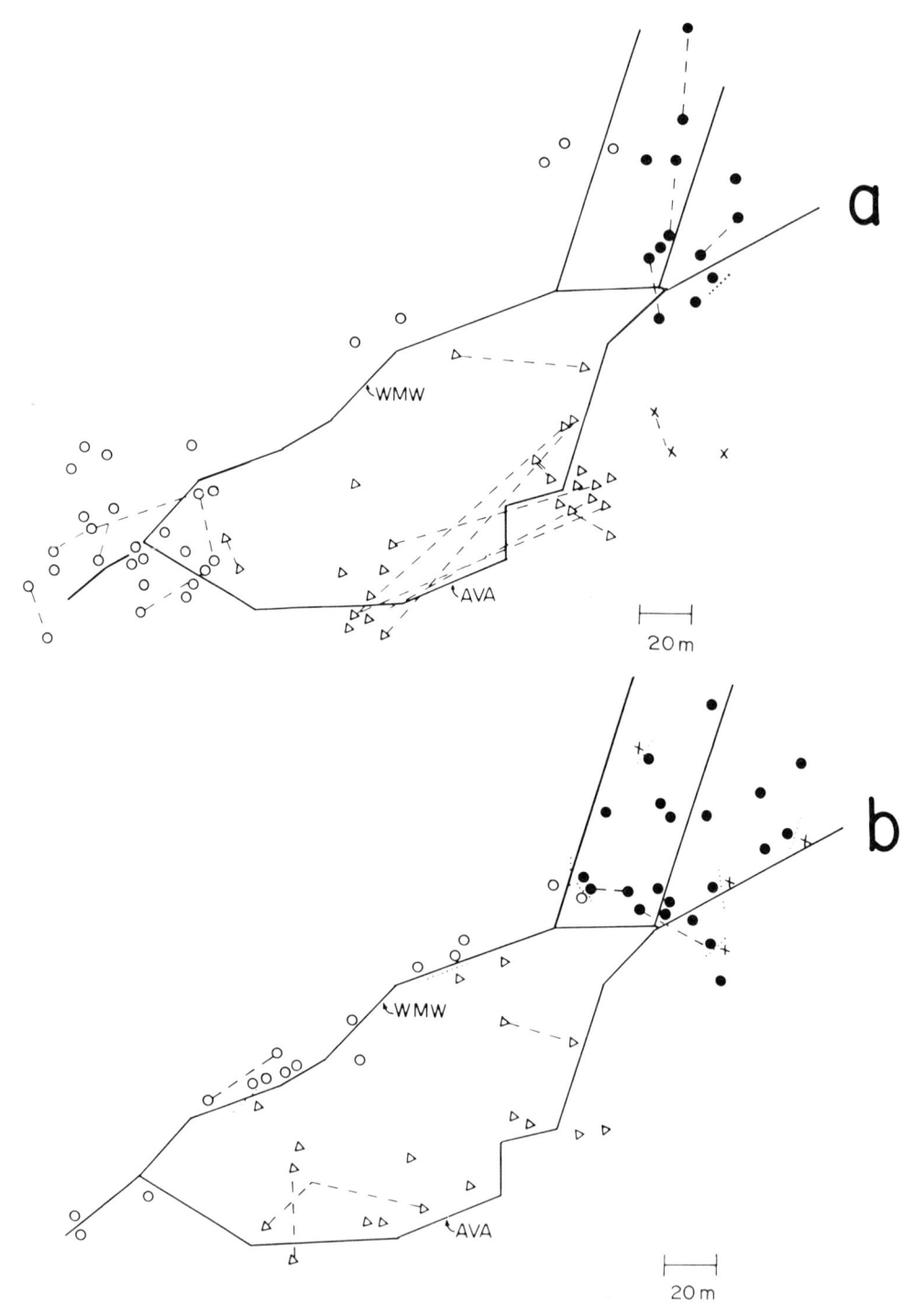

FIG. 11. The distribution of sightings of Chestnut-sided Warblers in the vicinity of the Armour-Wheeler junction trail on the BCI plateau during (a) 1977-1978 and (b) 1978-1979. Different symbols denote individuals, but similar symbols between years are not necessarily the same birds (in one case it definitely was not). All sightings are on separate days, unless connected by dashed lines.

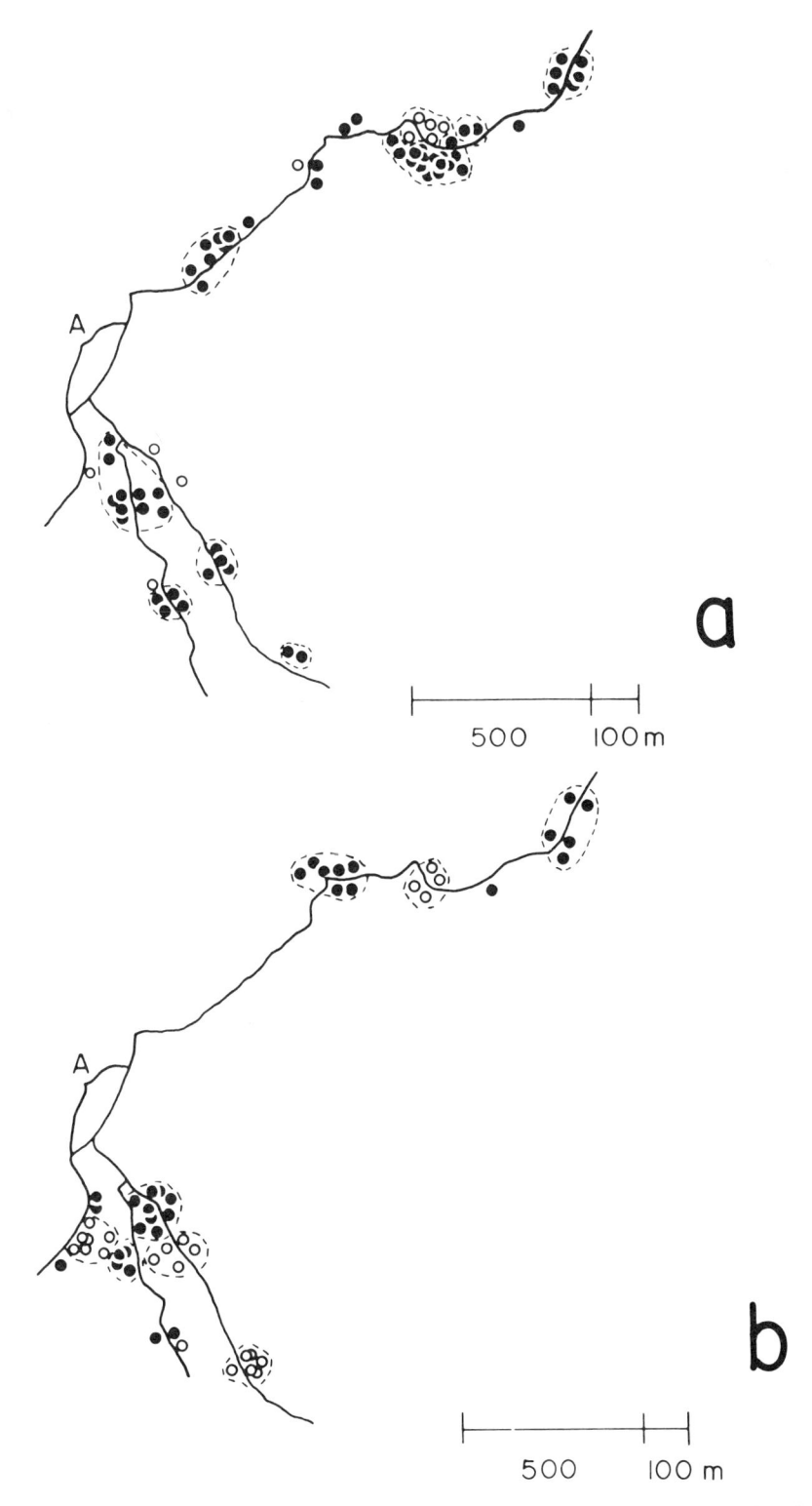

FIG. 12. The distribution of sightings of Chestnut-sided Warblers along the Snyder-Molino, Wheeler, and Drayton trail systems during (a, top) 1977-1978 and (b, bottom) 1978-1979. Dark dots denote probable adults and circles represent probable immatures. Dashed lines connect sightings that involve one bird (based on plumage). Omitted from this diagram are sightings in the vicinity of the trail loop presented in Figure 11 (indicated by "A"). In 1978-1979 the trail between Wheeler 9-12 was closed and not censused.

of the foraging birds had exposed markings (N = 20). Chestnut-sided Warblers when foraging hold the tail slightly cocked; in aggressive displays, however, the tail is often held straight out and the overall body posture is erect. Actual chasing is usually brief, seldom lasting more than 10-15 seconds.

Chestnut-sided Warblers in the BCI clearing responded to playbacks of their chip notes by giving rapid chip notes (Fig 13). They responded to rapid chips by approaching closely and giving soft high pitched zeet notes. These zeet notes preceded territorial chases in border interactions. Zeet notes might be particularly threatening at close range in dense vegetation since they have characteristics, such as long duration and narrow frequency range (Marler 1957), that should make the calling warbler difficult to locate. These call notes were not noted by Ficken and Ficken (1963) in their ethogram of the Chestnut-sided Warbler. I did not hear Chestnut-sided Warblers use chipping or zeeting in territorial interactions on their breeding grounds in Maine, nor have I heard other *Dendroica* use similar soft zeet notes.

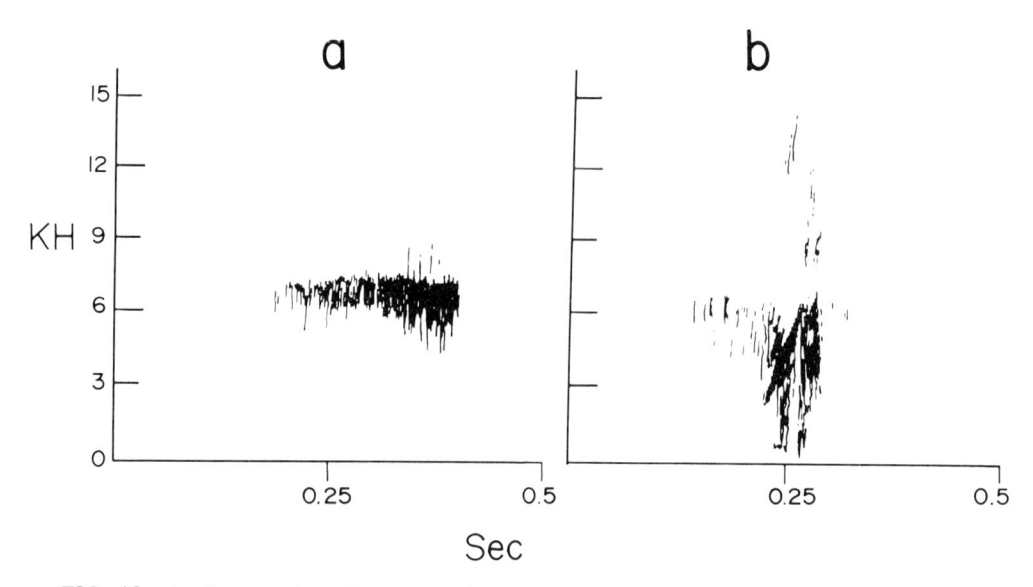

FIG 13. A diagram based on sound spectrographs of territorial call notes of the Chestnut-sided Warbler recorded during play back experiments. The two distinct calls are (a) a soft "zeet" note, given at close range, and (b) a chip.

THE BEHAVIOR OF WARBLERS AT ANTWREN FLOCKS

Unlike most of the warblers studied by Powell (1980), Chestnut-sided and Bay-breasted warblers followed mixed species flocks persistently. While Chestnut-sided Warblers ranked behind *Thamnophilus* in its frequency of attendance at the flock followed by Gradwohl and Greenberg (1980), the individual Chestnut-sided Warbler was the most persistent; several *Thamnophilus* pairs were involved. Even this frequency might be an underestimate; when the *Microrhopias* and the *Myrmotherula fulviventris* groups split up, the Chestnut-sided Warbler usually followed the *Microrhopias*; we generally followed *Myrmotherula*. Bay-breasted Warblers were less frequent both on the basis of how often the species occurred as a whole, and how frequently individual Bay-breasted Warblers were sighted. Individuals of both species appeared to follow the antwren flocks in bouts of similar length. The median minimum estimate of following was 60 minutes for both species (range = 5 - 180, U = 660, n.s.).

The high degree of co-occurrence of Chestnut-sided Warblers and canopy alliance species seems a paradox when the association between individual Chestnut-sided Warblers and antwren groups is known. Chestnut-sided Warblers only occur commonly with antwrens in certain portions of the antwren territories. They seem to avoid following the antwrens in the dense vine tangles which form the core of the antwren territory (Gradwohl and Greenberg 1980). They join the antwrens in the same areas as many other attendant species. In addition, when *Microrhopias* leaves the flocks, the Chestnut-sided Warbler usually follows them. This would explain the high degree of co-occurrence between these two species and the lack of co-occurence between Chestnut-sided Warbler and other antwrens.

WINTER FORAGING BEHAVIOR

FORAGING HEIGHT DISTRIBUTION

Bay-breasted Warblers tend to forage higher than Chestnut-sided Warblers in the BCI forest [$\bar{X}$ BBW = 55 ft (S.D. 25); $\bar{X}$ CSW = 41 (12)]. In addition, the foraging height distribution of the Bay-breasted Warbler is broader; it is more generalized with respect to its occurrence in forest strata (Fig. 14). Not only are the overall distributions based on observations from all three winters significantly different (X^2 = 56.75, d.f. = 4, p < .0001), but comparisons between species for each season are consistent; both Simpson index values, indicating foraging height niche breadths, and mean foraging height values were larger for the Bay-breasted Warbler for all seasons (U = 25, p < .05).

Whereas both species occur primarily in the upper branches of trees and shrubs (X^2 relative foraging height = 3.03, d.f. = 2, n.s.), Bay-breasted Warbler forages in larger trees (X^2 = 27.1, d.f. = 4, p < .001, tree height analyzed by same height intervals as foraging height). The tree height and relative foraging height data used in the chi-square analysis are presented in Fig. 15. While both species occur most commonly at mid-levels, the Bay-breasted Warbler was found more frequently in the upper stratum, particularly in the outer shell of canopy trees. This conclusion is supported by censuses conducted from the canopy tower on BCI 1978-1979 (Greenberg 1981c). Bay-breasted Warblers were 10 times more common than Chestnut-sided Warblers on this census, which is far greater than the 4:1 ratio found on ground-based censuses during the same year. The stronger preference for the outer canopy vegetation by the Bay-breasted Warbler is probably of great biological significance; the outer canopy is quite distinct, in terms of avifauna and environment, from the understory a few meters below. In fact, the outer canopy bird community has a much greater affinity with open second growth than with the forest understory (Orians 1961; Stiles 1980; Greenberg 1981c).

The two species respond quite differently to the difference in structure of the old and young forest on BCI (Fig. 16). The old forest tends to have a higher canopy and more even distribution of branches throughout the various strata. Young forest is of lower stature and has high branch density in the mid-stratum (31-50 ft.). Chestnut-sided Warbler had the same foraging height distribution across these habitats; whereas, Bay-breasted Warbler had a significantly different distribution (X^2 = 62.2, d.f. = 4, p < .01). The Bay-breasted Warbler distributions were remarkably similar to the distribution of branches in the same

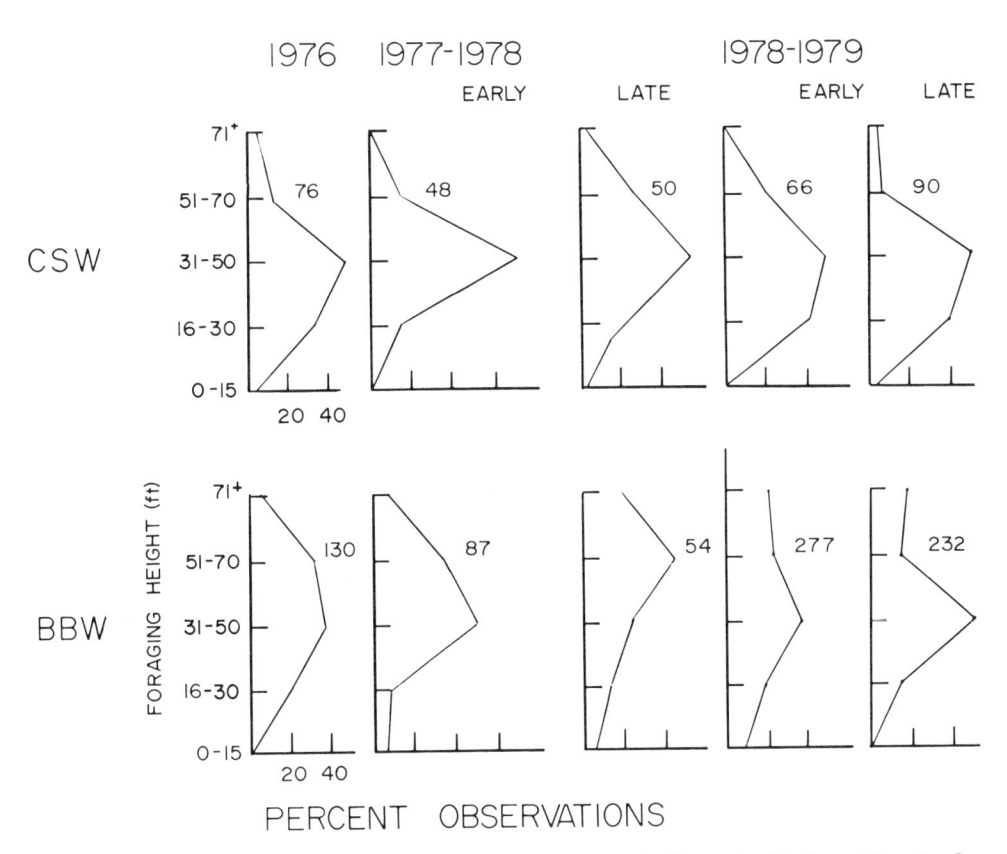

FIG. 14. Proportion of sightings for Bay-breasted and Chestnut-sided warblers in five foraging height strata on BCI. Data for 1977–1979 are presented in approximate half winter intervals corresponding to late wet-early dry season and mid- to late dry seasons (October-31 December and 1 January-April). Sample sizes are indicated by each graph.

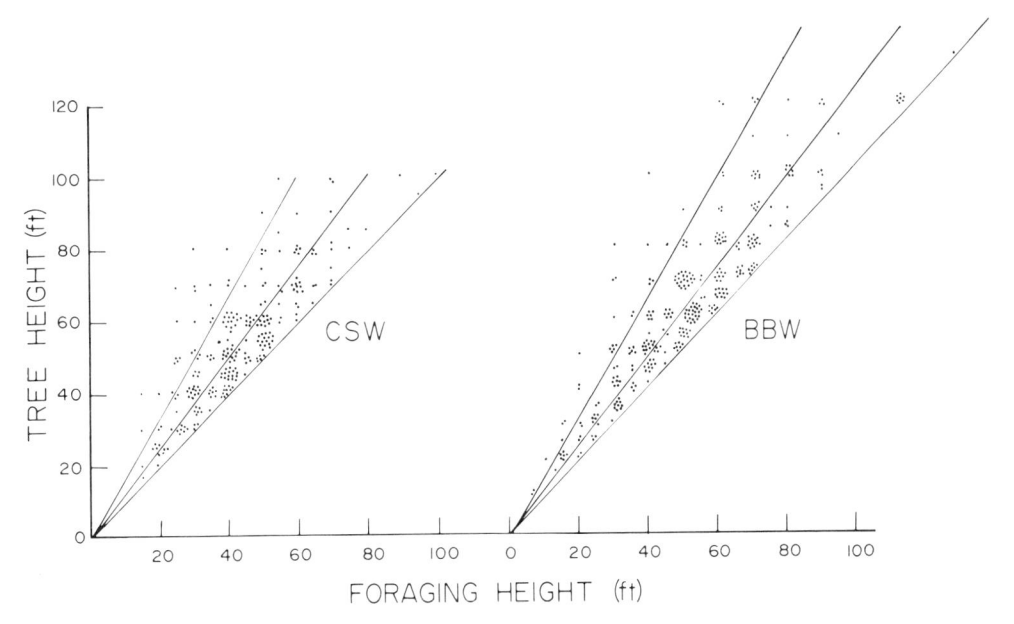

FIG. 15. Scatter diagrams of foraging height versus height of the tree in which the Chestnut-sided and Bay-breasted warblers were foraging. Solid lines indicate points at which the bird would be at 60%, 80%, and 100% of the height of the tree. (These categories are used in chi-square analysis of relative tree height).

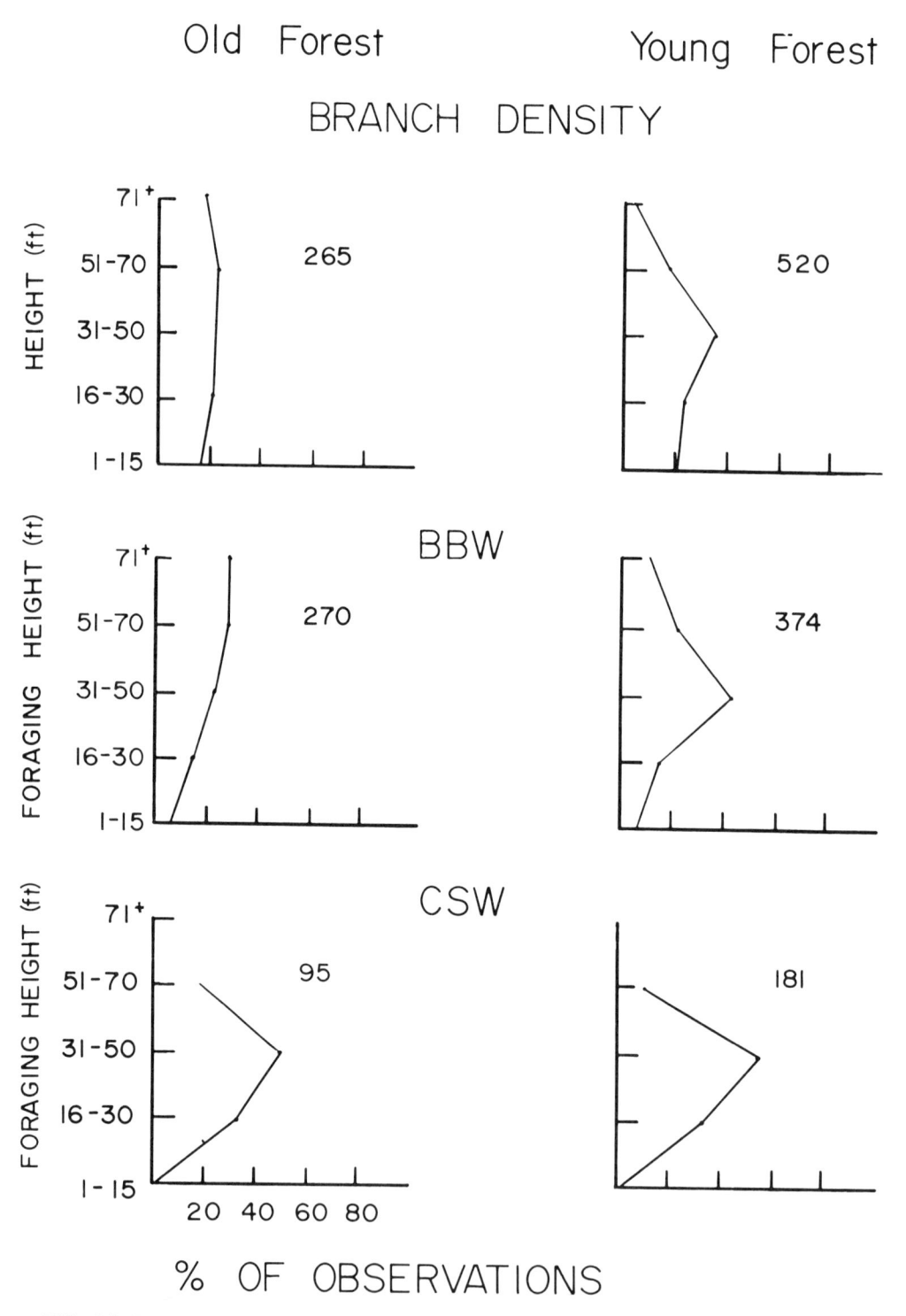

FIG. 16. Foraging height distribution of Bay-breasted and Chestnut-sided warblers and the density of branches across five strata in the BCI old and young forest. Branch densities are based on foliage surveys outlined in Methods. Sample sizes of foraging observations or branch numbers are indicated by each graph.

forest type. Chestnut-sided Warbler foraging height distribution was similar to the branch distribution in young forest, but radically different from the branch distribution in old forest. One reason that Chestnut-sided Warblers may not have tracked changes in the structure of the vegetation is that Chestnut-sided Warblers are found locally in disturbed portions of the old forest. In these areas, poorly represented in random branch density surveys, branch distribution is probably more similar to young forest.

It is puzzling that Chestnut-sided Warblers are not more common in the sunny canopy, which is more similar in some ways than is the somber forest understory to the open scrub habitat in which they breed. This is all the more difficult to understand, since Chestnut-sided Warblers are relatively numerous in open, second-growth habitats in Central America. The scarcity of Chestnut-sided Warblers in the outer canopy may be a result of low branch density in this stratum. The foraging behavior of the Chestnut-sided Warbler involves rapid branch changes (see Foraging Behavior), which may be difficult in the crown of a large canopy tree. Bay-breasted Warblers often forage by working along branches and may not be so limited. In the mature forest at La Selva, Costa Rica, I found most of the Chestnut-sided Warblers to be concentrated at greater heights than BCI (60-80 ft). In this taller, wetter forest, the stratum of highest branch density is shifted upward.

The Chestnut-sided Warbler is most similar to *Microrhopias* and *Hylophilus* in its foraging height distribution (Fig. 17). The Bay-breasted Warbler is very similar to *Dacnis* and *Tachyphonus*. *Myrmotherula axillaris* is distinct from all other foliage-gleaners on BCI in that it occurs commonly in the low open understory. It is joined by *Hylophilus ochraceiceps* in wetter and higher elevation forests on the nearby mainland.

FORAGING SUBSTRATE

The Bay-breasted Warbler is far more diverse in the surfaces from which it captures arthropods than is the Chestnut-sided Warbler (Table 19). The Chestnut-sided Warbler is specialized on foliage insectivory, directing approximately 93% of its maneuvers towards leaf surfaces (range 90-94% for each season). The Bay-breasted Warbler, however, is far less restricted to capturing arthropods from leaves. The overall mean for foliage insectivory across all seasons was 71% (52-87%). The most important alternative substrates for both species are twigs and branches.

Even within foliage insectivory, the two species show profound differences. Chestnut-sided Warblers are restricted to capturing prey off the undersurfaces of leaves; whereas, the Bay-breasted Warbler is more generalized in its leaf surface use (Greenberg and Gradwohl 1980b). In the Chestnut-sided Warbler 90% (seasonal range 87-96) of all foraging maneuvers to leaves were to the undersurface; in the Bay-breasted Warbler, this figure was only 60% (seasonal range 44-75%). The difference in overall substrate use is highly significant ($X^2 = 155$, d.f. = 4, $p < .0001$).

The Bay-breasted Warbler showed more distinct seasonal variation in foraging substrate use. In the wet season, it foraged more off the upper than the lower

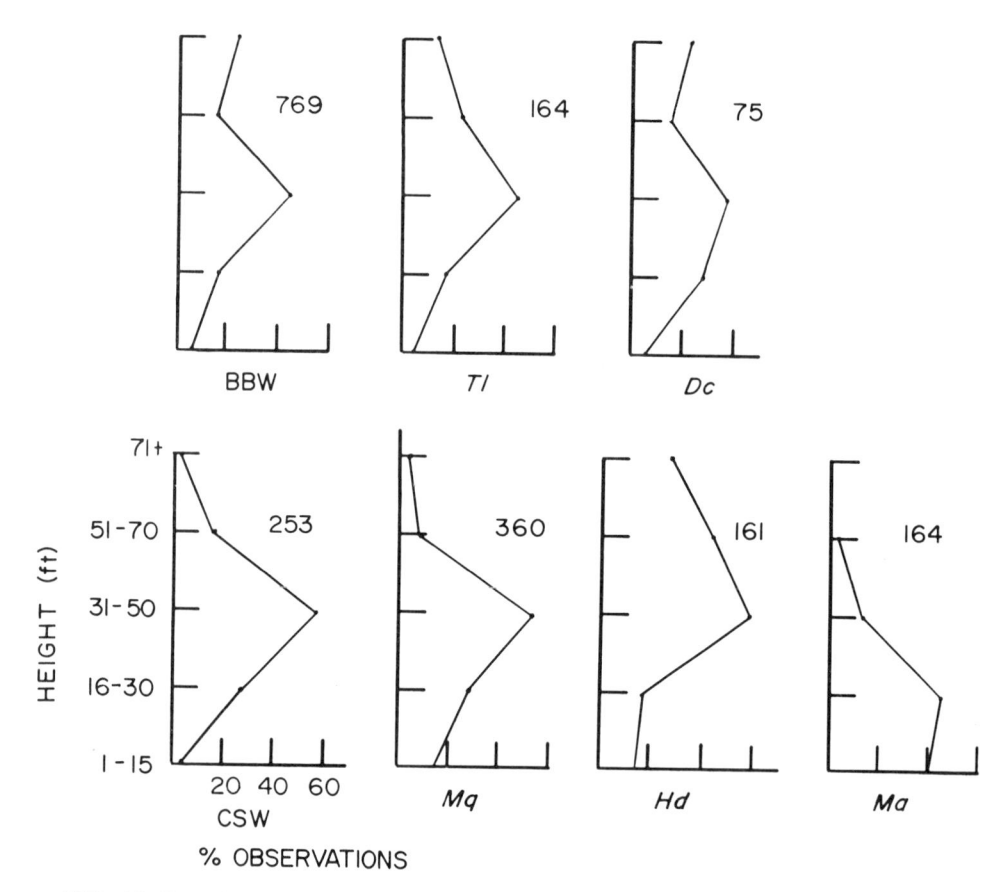

FIG. 17. Foraging height distributions of the BCI foliage-gleaning species. Sample sizes are indicated by each graph. See Table 15 for abbreviations.

surfaces of leaves; in the dry season, the Bay-breasted Warblers concentrated more on leaf undersurfaces. Bay-breasted Warblers appeared to be tracking changes in the available resources. During the dry season, arthropods are more restricted to leaf undersurfaces (Greenberg and Gradwohl 1980b). The Chestnut-sided Warbler, like other BCI foliage-gleaning birds, shows little shift in insectivorous foraging microhabitat from season to season.

The two warblers are more similar to other species of foliage gleaners than they are to each other, in terms of the foraging surface used. The Chestnut-sided Warbler is similar to the antwrens *Microrhopias* and *Myrmotherula axillaris* and the greenlet *Hylophilus decurtatus* (Table 19) in its concentration on leaf undersurfaces. The Bay-breasted Warbler is intermediate between these leaf undersurface foragers and the upper surface foragers *Tachyphonus* and *Dacnis*. *Dacnis*, however, often probes into leaf curls and pecks into areas of leaf damage (Greenberg and Gradwohl 1980b). *Myrmotherula* and the Bay-breasted Warbler are the two species least committed to capturing arthropods off leaf surfaces.

Table 19. Foraging substrates of foliage-gleaning birds on BCI

Species	N	Leaf Bottom	Leaf Top	Leaf Total	Twig	Air	Dead Leaf	Other
Myrmotherula axillaris	150	.64	.18	.82	.09	.01	.09	0
Microrhopias quixensis	181	.80	.14	.94	.03	0	.01	0
Hylophilus decurtatus	105	.74	.15	.89	.03	.01	.07	0
Dacnis cayana	65	.30	.70	1.00	0	0	0	0
Tachyphonus luctuosus	75	.14	.75	.89	.04	.08	0	0
Bay-breasted Warbler								
early 1977-78[a]	171	.38	.49	.87	.08	.03	0	0
late 1977-78[b]	71	.39	.13	.52	.32	.04	.05	.05
early 1978-79	137	.34	.35	.69	.87	.08	.03	0
late 1978-79	96	.50	.22	.72	.18	.01	.06	.01
Grand Total[c]	475	.41	.30	.71	.21	.03	.04	.01
Chestnut-sided Warbler								
early 1977-78	108	.81	.13	.94	.03	.02	.01	0
late 1977-78	71	.85	.11	.96	.03	.01	0	0
early 1978-79	97	.83	.11	.94	.04	0	0	0
late 1978-79	86	.87	.03	.90	.08	0	.01	0
Total	362	.84	.09	.93	.04	.01	.01	0

a. Early is from October to 31 December. b. Late is from 1 January to May.
c. Grand means of all seasons

FOLIAGE ARRANGEMENTS AROUND FORAGING WARBLERS

Leaf arrangements and branch orientation determine the visibility of leaf surfaces around foraging birds (Greenberg and Gradwohl 1980b; Holmes and Robinson 1981). Tropical forest, with its myriad of plant growth forms, provides a complex array of foliage arrangements. It seems reasonable that different species of foliage gleaning birds might use different leaf arrangements, and such interspecific differences are in fact evident (Table 20).

Planar leaf arrangements predominate in lowland tropical forest vegetation and are commonly used by all species of foliage-gleaning bird. The Chestnut-sided Warbler is particularly restricted to these sorts of arrangements (71%); whereas the Bay-breasted Warbler is less specialized (53%) on these horizontally-oriented sprays ($X^2 = 8.4$, d.f. = 1, $p < .01$). This may be a conservative estimate of the difference. These data were gathered in the dry season (1978-1979); Bay-breasted Warblers were less diverse in their foliage arrangement use during this period. *Hylophilus decurtatus* and *Myrmotherula axillaris* share the Chestnut-sided Warblers' restriction to planar structures, whereas *Tachyphonus luctuosus* and *Microrhopias* are similar to the Bay-breasted Warbler.

Of the species that use alternate arrangements with great frequency, the Bay-breasted Warbler and *Microrhopias* are found particularly commonly in vertically oriented vines. *Tachyphonus*, however, is found more commonly in clustered (i.e., *Gustavia*) or palm foliage than are other species.

Foliage arrangement types are not randomly distributed throughout the forest. They vary in frequency between old and young forest and between the understory and canopy (Leigh 1975). For example, orthotropic arrangements tend to be more common in canopy trees, and palm foliage is found predominantly in the understory. Differences in leaf arrangements used by different species should be expected simply on the basis of different foraging height distributions. In light of this, the extreme difference between the Chestnut-sided Warbler and *Microrhopias*, two species with nearly identical foraging height distributions and a strong behavioral association, is of particular interest.

To isolate foliage-type selection from variation in foraging height distribution for other species, I compared the leaf arrangement distribution of each species to an expected distribution. This expected distribution was based on the vertical distribution of different leaf arrangements and the foraging height distribution of each foliage-gleaner. While these data are subject to error and potential bias, they do indicate that the fine scale structure of the foraging microhabitat of foliage-gleaning birds can be characterized beyond mere vertical stratification.

Since the distribution of leaf arrangements is quite distinct between young and old forest, I have restricted my analysis to data gathered in the young forest of BCI. Table 21 presents the number of branches, with the different leaf arrangements found at the five strata of the young forest. To generate the expected values of a given leaf arrangement used by a particular species, I took the product of the proportion of branches comprising a single leaf arrangement type in one stratum and the proportion of total foraging observations for a bird species in that stratum; these values were summed for all strata. Expected and observed values are presented in Table 22 along with X^2 values comparing each

Table 20. Percent use of various leaf arrangements by foliage-gleaning birds on BCI

Species	N	Planar[a]	Semi[a]	Orthotropic Tree	Orthotropic Vine	Palm Tree	Clustered Tree	Apposition Tree
Myrmotherula axillaris	77	43	13	24	9	2	10	0
Microrhopias quixensis	130	72	4	9	5	1	8	0
Hylophilus decurtatus	91	60	10	7	9	0	9	5
Bay-breasted Warbler	102	42	10	21	17	2	6	2
Chestnut-sided Warbler	95	59	13	19	4	0	2	3
Tachyphonus luctuosus	66	48	6	14	6	8	18	2

a. Tree or vine.

Table 21. The available foliage arrangements in young forest on BCI, based on 150 samples at random points along trails

Strata	Planar	Orthotropic Tree	Vine	Palm	Total
71+ feet	.36	.64	0	0	22
51-70	.59	.34	.07	0	103
31-50	.49	.40	.08	.04	166
6-30	.72	.19	.06	.03	121
1-15	.64	.20	.03	.13	108

Table 22. Chi-square analysis of the use of foliage arrangements in the young forest of BCI versus available foliage arrangements within the foraging height distribution of foliage-gleaning birds

Species	Chi-square	p	Major departure from expected
Microrhopias quixensis		n.s.	
Myrmotherula axillaris	18.4	.001	Prefers planar arrangements
Hylophilus decurtatus	19.9	.001	Prefers planar arrangements
Chestnut-sided Warbler	8.4	.001	Prefers planar arrangements
Bay-breasted Warbler		n.s.	
Tachyphonus luctuosus		n.s.	(heavy use of palms)

species with its expected value (ignoring variables with cells that have an expected value less than five).

Nonrandom use of foliage types was found for three species: the Chestnut-sided Warbler and *Hylophilus* were significantly associated with planar arrangements; *Myrmotherula axillaris* avoided orthotropic vine or palm foliage. The three species associated with nonplanar arrangements showed no significant departure from the available foliage in their foraging height distributions.

The explanation for the difference from expected foliage arrangement use is not known. Foraging birds could easily "select" particular plant types to forage in as they move through a tropical forest, since so many different plant types are intermingled. Alternatively, these departures may reflect differences in horizontal distribution similar to differences in vertical distribution already explored. Different foliage arrangements may have their own characteristic distribution with respect to disturbance in the forest. This is most obviously true with vine foliage, which tends to be most common in old light gaps. The high degree of co-occurrence of these species in mixed flocks should minimize the effect of spatial segregation on foliage arrangement use.

A possible functional explanation for foliage arrangement specialization is that prey attack between branches is easier if branches are horizontally arranged. Nonplanar arrangements should obscure upward vision and maneuverability (Greenberg and Gradwohl 1980b). The Chestnut-sided Warbler and *Hylophilus* show the strongest avoidance of nonplanar foliage and the greatest frequency of interbranch attacks (see Foraging Attack Behavior). The Chestnut-sided Warbler and *Hylophilus* undertake such attacks 36% and 60% of all attacks respectively; whereas, this value is 25% for *Tachyphonus*, 22% for Bay-breasted Warbler, 21% for *Microrhopias*, 14% for *Myrmotherula axillaris*, and 0% for *Dacnis*.

OTHER FORAGING MICROHABITAT VARIABLES

Perch size. Bay-breasted and Chestnut-sided warblers were indistinguishable in the distribution of perch sizes used (Table 23). Among foliage-gleaners on BCI, however, I found a considerable range in the proportion of use of large perches (> 1 cm). *Tachyphonus* was found on larger branches 40% of the time, whereas *Dacnis* was found only on small perches. The basic foraging style of *Dacnis* probably makes it incomparable to the other foliage-gleaners. Dacnises fly directly to leaves showing obvious insect damage and perch on the petioles as they attempt to extract the larvae. Their foraging does not generally involve active hopping from perch to perch within trees.

Among the species that move continuously from branch to branch within trees, the size of branch used appears to be correlated with body size. The larger foliage-gleaners use larger branches more often. While this suggests that small body size may be related, in part, to specialization on small branches, this suggestion is tentative; the only significant interspecific differences are between *Tachyphonus* and all other species, and between the Bay-breasted Warbler and *Microrhopias* (X^2 test, d.f. = 2, p < .05).

Leaf Size. The various gleaners display little specialization on leaves of different sizes (Table 24). The square root of the product of length and width of leaves of

Table 23. The distribution of perch sizes used by foliage-gleaning birds on BCI

Species	Branch size classes (mm)					
	0-10	11-20	21-30	31-40	41-50	51+
Myrmotherula axillaris (49)	92%	4%	2%	2%	0%	0%
Microrhopias quixensis (50)	84	10	2	2	0	0
Hylophilus decurtatus (46)	89	7	4	0	2	0
Chestnut-sided Warbler (153)	81	12	3	0	2	2
Bay-breasted Warbler (290)	76	10	5	1	4	4
Dacnis cayana (25)	100	0	0	0	0	0
Tachyphonus luctuosus (35)	63	21	8	0	5	3

plants in which I found foliage-gleaners ranged from 4-5.1 inches. Chestnut-sided and Bay-breasted warblers used, on the average, the smallest leaves probably because they avoid the foliage of megaphyllous plants such as *Gustavia superba*. But the only difference between the Chestnut-sided Warbler and *Tachyphonus* is significant (T = 2.5, p < .05).

Canopy Cover. The degree of canopy cover over foraging birds varied substantially from 52% cover over *Dacnis* and *Tachyphonus* to a somber 81% cover over *Myrmotherula axillaris* (Table 25). This gradient probably reflects the preferred foraging strata of the different species; canopy species have a lower mean cover than understory species. Bay-breasted Warbler has a mean canopy cover value approaching the canopy tanagers, whereas the Chestnut-sided Warbler is similar to the mid-level insectivores.

FORAGING BEHAVIOR

Attack Behavior. Bay-breasted and Chestnut-sided warblers differ in the degree to which simple gleaning is used to capture insects (Table 26, X^2 = 19.5, d.f. = 1, p < .001). The Bay-breasted Warbler gleans about two-thirds of the time, versus only one-half in the Chestnut-sided Warbler. Both species hover glean in similar frequency, but the rapid leaping motion is more characteristic of the Chestnut-sided Warbler.

Other foliage-gleaning birds tend to concentrate on gleaning. Greenlets, however, leap and hang on leaf undersurfaces over 50% of the time. The two antwrens are more similar to the Bay-breasted than Chestnut-sided Warbler in their predominant use of gleaning. This is surprising since the Chestnut-sided Warbler is more similar in microhabitat use (e.g., leaf undersurface specialization)

Table 24. Leaf size index (square root of product of length and width) of plants in which individuals of BCI foliage-gleaners were observed

Species	N	Size (in)
Myrmotherula axillaris	53	4.8 (3.7)[a]
Microrhopias quixensis	48	4.4 (2.2)
Hylophilus decurtatus	53	4.8 (2.5)
Chestnut-sided Warbler	154	4.1 (1.7)
Bay-breasted Warbler	188	4.2 (1.9)
Tachyphonus luctuosus	56	5.1 (2.8)

a. Mean + standard deviation in parentheses.

Table 25. Percentage of crown cover over foraging individuals of BCI foliage-gleaning birds

Species	N	% Crown Cover
Myrmotherula axillaris	50	81.0 (2.1)
Microrhopias quixensis	45	64.4 (3.8)[a]
Hylophilus decurtatus	55	67.8 (2.3)
Chestnut-sided Warbler	148	67.0 (5.2)
Bay-breasted Warbler	221	59.2 (1.8)
Dacnis cayana	25	52.4 (6.0)
Tachyphonus luctuosus	60	52.0 (2.5)

a. Mean + standard error in parentheses.

to these antwrens than is the Bay-breasted Warbler. Moreover, *Tachyphonus*, a leaftop forager (Table 19), employs many active prey attack techniques, particularly hover-gleaning and lunging. *Dacnis*, also a leaftop forager, is the least active in its attack behavior. While some 30% of its foraging consists of hanging on the undersurface of a leaf or petiole, this is done by leaning over on the same branch, rather than leaping to a branch overhead as in *Hylophilus*. These results suggest that leaf surface specialization does not relate to how active the attack method is for a foliage-gleaning species, as suggested in Greenberg and Gradwohl (1980b). Other features of foraging ecology, such as locomotor patterns, are probably more important.

Locomotor Patterns. Bay-breasted and Chestnut-sided warblers are easily distinguished by the way they move through foliage. Bay-breasted Warblers move deliberately, slowly wagging their tails through a shallow 15 degree arc. Chestnut-sided Warblers hop about actively, wings often slightly drooped and tail cocked about 35 degrees over the plane of the back.

The more deliberate movement of Bay-breasted Warblers has been frequently noted (Bent 1953; MacArthur 1958; Morton 1980). But Bay-breasted Warblers are not necessarily sluggish and vireo-like. Often they move rapidly and cover great distances. On Barro Colorado Island (BCI), I found they move frequently, but cover only slightly smaller distances when all foraging movements are summed (19 versus 31 ft./min.), and they move as frequently as the Chestnut-sided Warbler (Table 27). The major difference between the two species is that the Chestnut-sided Warbler hops and flies between branches; whereas, the Bay-breasted Warbler generally moves along branches. The differences in the ratio of movements along branches to branch changes is significant whether distance or frequency of movement is considered (Table 27). In addition, the Chestnut-sided Warbler uses its wings in short flights more often.

Table 26. Foraging tactics (attack method) of foliage-gleaning birds on Barro Colorado Island (BCI)

Species	Glean	Knock	Lean	Hover	Leap	Lunge	Sally	Hang
Myrmotherula axillaris (98)	.68	.02	0	.05	.09	.06	.01	.08
Microrhopias quixensis (109)	.65	.02	0	.02	.10	.09	.03	.08
Hylophilus decurtatus (109)	.39	0	0	.04	0	.01	0	.56
Chestnut-sided Warbler (361)	.50	.01	0	.17	.25	.04	.01	.01
Bay-breasted Warbler (496)	.65	.01	0	.20	.05	.08	.01	0
Dacnis cayana (50)	.74	0	.22	0	0	.02	.02	0
Tachyphonus luctuosus (70)	.42	0	0	.24	.03	.25	.05	0

Table 27. Locomotory patterns of Bay-breasted and Chestnut-sided Warblers on BCI

Movement Variable	Chestnut-sided (32 ind., 6030 sec.)	Bay-breasted (30 ind., 5000 sec.)	U	P
Branch change/no. creep movements	0.45 (0.06)[a]	1.31 (0.08)	830	.001
Branch change/creep distance (ft)	0.11 (0.02)	0.57 (0.09)	830	.001
Branch change/min.[b]	15.7 (0.8)	11.7 (1.2)	763	.001
Creep/min.	9.2 (0.7)	18.5 (1.4)	720	.001
Hops/min.	13.0 (0.7)	9.4 (0.7)	715	.001
Flights/min.	3.0 (0.3)	2.5 (0.3)	756	.001
Total distance/min. (ft)[c]	30.7 (2.0)	19.4 (1.4)	810	.001

a. Mean for all individuals, s.e. in parentheses.
b. Includes flights and hops.
c. Sum of the distance of all movements, excluding flights over 15 feet.

When searching foliage, Chestnut-sided Warblers stare continuously with their head oriented in an upward direction, presumably examining the undersurface of leaves on overhead branches. Bay-breasted Warblers, however, tend to peer about slowly (also see Morton 1980). I classified the direction of search with respect to a vertical plane (e.g., up, level, down) every 10 seconds for 50 seconds in 35 individuals of each species. The up:level:down percentages for the Chestnut-sided Warbler were 68:11:21 and for the Bay-breasted Warbler were 46:25:27. Chestnut-sided Warblers concentrate their search more; the mean Simpson index for the Bay-breasted Warbler was 2.3 versus 1.54 in the Chestnut-sided Warbler, which is significantly different ($U_{(35,35)}$ = 1162, p < .001).

While I did not track other foliage-gleaning birds on BCI in the same manner, *Hylophilus*, *Microrhopias*, and *Myrmotherula axillaris* forage by active branch changing in a manner similar to the Chestnut-sided Warbler. *Tachyphonus* often hops along branches, flicking its wings. *Dacnis*, on the other hand, rarely move systematically through a tree, but fly directly to areas with leaf curls or damage.

OPPORTUNISTIC FORAGING IN BAY-BREASTED WARBLERS

Within the context of a tropical rain forest, Bay-breasted Warblers are remarkably generalized in where they search for insects. Still, observations made in other habitats reveal a degree of foraging plasticity reminiscent of Yellow-rumped Warblers. In suburban settings in Panama, Bay-breasted Warblers are often seen foraging in small groups on lawns and road shoulders. I observed several foraging for insects off the dog food offered to Coatis in the Summit Garden Zoo. Bay-breasted (and Tennessee) Warblers commonly forage off buildings near insect-attracting lights in the BCI clearing. Most Bay-breasted Warblers in the clearing forage off buildings and screens and do so from the day of their arrival in late October and early November. Chestnut-sided Warblers wintering in the BCI clearing were observed to forage at this abundant source of arthropods on only two occasions during the three winters. Chestnut-sided Warblers were undoubtedly morphologically capable of foraging off screens, as no obvious morphological features are required to hover or grab at the screening. It is possible that they are less exploratory of novel foraging situations. The basis for this propensity of Bay-breasted Warblers to forage in a wide variety of situations could be examined employing experiments with caged birds. In the case of the BCI clearing, the difference is not the age structure of the population (young Bay-breasted Warblers showing plastic behavior); the adult:immature ratio was approximately 50:50 for both species.

FRUGIVORY IN WARBLERS

General Pattern in Warbler frugivory. Bay-breasted and Chestnut-sided warblers both eat fruit (see also Morton 1980), but the Bay-breasted Warbler was far more frequently observed at fruiting trees (Greenberg 1981a). Both warblers showed the same seasonal pattern of frugivory (Fig. 18 a,b), but in the Bay-breasted Warbler 20-25% of all observations were of frugivorous individuals, as opposed to only 5% for the Chestnut-sided Warbler.

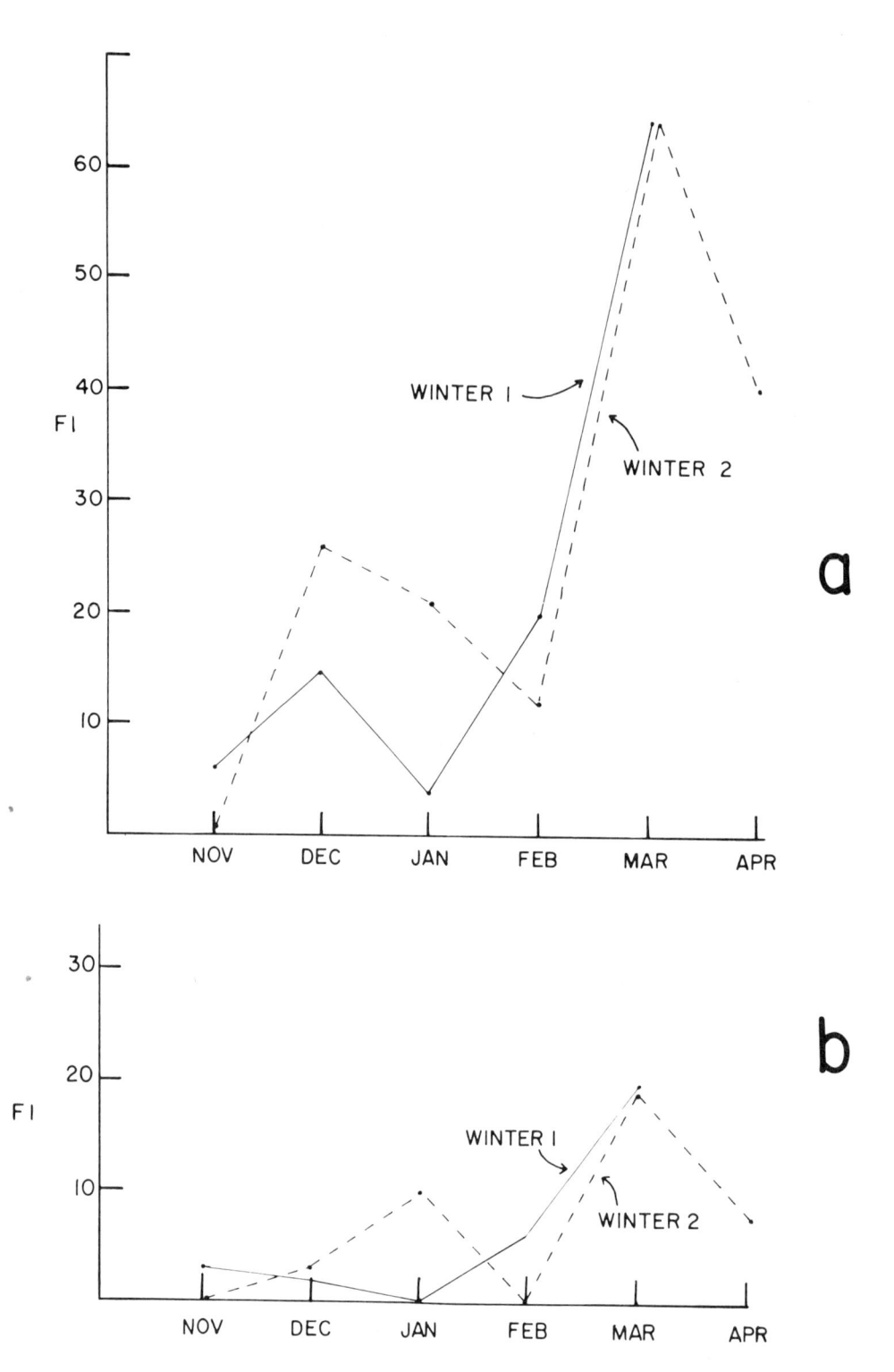

FIG. 18. The "Frugivory Index," approximately the proportion of warblers observed foraging on fruit per month (Greenberg 1981), for Chestnut-sided and Bay-breasted warblers in (a) 1977-1978 and (b) 1978-1979.

The frequency of frugivory in Bay-breasted Warbler falls between, and is significantly different than, that of *Tachyphonus* (X^2 = 12.9, d.f. = 1, p < .001) and *Dacnis* (X^2 = 10.25, d.f. = 1, p < .001) (Table 28). The Chestnut-sided Warbler, on the other hand, slightly (and insignificantly) exceeded the degree of frugivory found in *Hylophilus*. The antwrens are strict insectivores, never taking fruit and nectar.

Bay-breasted and Chestnut-sided warblers share similar preferences in fruiting tree species. Both warblers visited only a few species, concentrating primarily on *Miconia argentia* and *Lindackeria laurina*, and to a lesser degree on the small fruited *Casearia* (*sylvestris* and *arborea*). Other small frugivorous birds visit far more species of fruiting plants on BCI (pers. obs., A. Worthington pers. comm.) and Trinidad (Snow 1962a, b; Snow and Snow 1971).

Characteristics of Warbler Preferred Fruits. The two preferred trees produce quite different fruits. *Lindackeria* has a rich, waxy, red aril (0.04 g dry wt) attached to a relatively large seed (0.02 g), one or several of which are contained in a soft-spiny green capsule. *Miconia argentia* produces a copious crop of small green berries that ripen to a dark purple (0.02 g dry wt). In fact, small size is the only feature that characterizes warbler preferred fruit. The gape of *Dendroica* is only 5-7 mm. Even this does not set a strict limit on the size of fruit eaten; warblers take small bites from the soft aril of *Lindackeria*, and Tennessee Warblers probe and gape into *Miconia* berries.

The two fruits are phenologically distinct. *Lindackeria* arils first appear irregularly between December and March. Within a year, the crop of different trees is poorly synchronized (pers. obs.; A. Worthington pers. comm.; Foster 1973). *Miconia argentia* produces a well synchronized crop in March or April that usually lasts into June.

Table 28. Percentage of individuals feeding on plant material (primarily fruit)

Species	N	Percentage Omnivory[a]
Myrmotherula axillaris	750	0
Microrhopias quixensis	1123	0
Hylophilus decurtatus	374	1
Chestnut-sided Warbler	410	6
Tachyphonus luctuosus	223	12
Bay-breasted Warbler	1311	22
Dacnis cayana	105	36

a. Similarity to frugivory index (Greenberg 1981a), but includes observations of nectarivory.

The two fruits are nutritional opposites. *Miconia* is 98% water versus only 49% for *Lindackeria*. In addition, *Lindackeria* is lipid rich (55% dry wt), whereas *Miconia* contains little of energetic value besides non-structural carbohydrates (Table 29). *Lindackeria*, in fact, contains more lipid than most fruits (McDiarmid et al. 1977; Milton pers. comm.) and is equivalent to the oily palm fruits preferred by oilbirds. Several other small bird-dispersed fruits have been shown to have very high lipid content (McDiarmid et al. 1977; Stiles 1980). Because of this high fat and low moisture content, *Lindackeria* is a high calorie meal. A gram of *Lindackeria* aril has a minimum of 5.5 Kcal (crude protein not included) versus 1.2 Kcal in *Miconia* pulp. Caloric content was calculated with the following formula (Paine 1971): Kcal/g fruit = (9.5 × g lipid) ÷ g fruit + 4.1 g nonstructural carbohydrates ÷ g fruit.

The species composition of visitors to the two trees was radically different (see Greenberg 1981a). *Lindackeria* received warbler visits almost to the exclusion of other species. Tennessee Warblers, a rare bird on BCI, were common at *Lindackeria*. Most small omnivorous tanagers and honeycreepers were absent. Although *Miconia* received warbler visits out of proportion to warbler abundance among small omnivores on BCI, all resident omnivores visited the tree frequently (50 species).

Miconia and molt in Dendroica. During March and early April, most Bay-breasted and many Chestnut-sided warblers can be found in and around fruiting *Miconia argentia* (see Morton 1980). The period of association with *Miconia* is the period of most intense frugivory in *Dendroica* in the Canal Area (Greenberg 1981a). In addition, this period precedes migration and coincides with an intense period of body molt.

Molt is the primary productive activity of wintering warblers. It is presumably the period of greatest energy and protein demands during the stay of warblers on

Table 29. The nutritional composition of two preferred fruits of Warblers on BCI (Values are percent dry weight)

Species	Sample	N	Lipids	TNC[a]
Miconia argentea	ripe + seeds (3 samples)	1.0-1.1	1.5-2.9	17.9-37.7
	unripe + seeds	0.7	3.9	17.1
	seeds[b] (2 samples)	2.3-2.5	0.1	0.1
Lindackeria laurina	aril	?	53.0	14.3

a. Total non-structural carbohydrates.
b. Seeds comprise 16% of the total dry weight of the berries.

BCI. During molt of the body feather coat, 25% of the non-skeletal dry weight of a Bay-breasted Warbler, primarily keratinized protein, is totally replaced (data from one dried and dissected warbler from BCI). Body molt in these warblers is particularly intense since it occurs rapidly; during the peak of molt, birds are mostly covered with pin- feathers (Morton 1980). I examined the seasonal extent of molt (Fig. 19) by classifying observed warblers into different molt categories. This is easily done in Bay-breasted Warblers, which molt from a largely dull olive plumage to a largely rufous (male) or cinnamon-buff (female) plumage. The initiation of molt can be determined, at close range through binoculars, by the presence of dark feathers among the olive; the cessation of molt is determined when no olive feathers can be detected in the chestnut or buff on the crown, breast, or upper sides. My subsequent experience with captive Bay-breasted Warblers suggests that this field scoring of molt is quite accurate. Individuals in detectable molt were observed for six weeks in 1978-1979. The time from the first sign of molt in the first molting individuals to the first completely molted individual was three and one-half weeks. Body molt in most temperate zone passerines lasts at least five weeks; in tropical passerines it is presumably slower (Payne 1972).

The peak in frugivory corresponds to the peak in molt (Figs. 18 & 19). The decline in frugivory in April is particularly interesting since *Miconia* fruits into

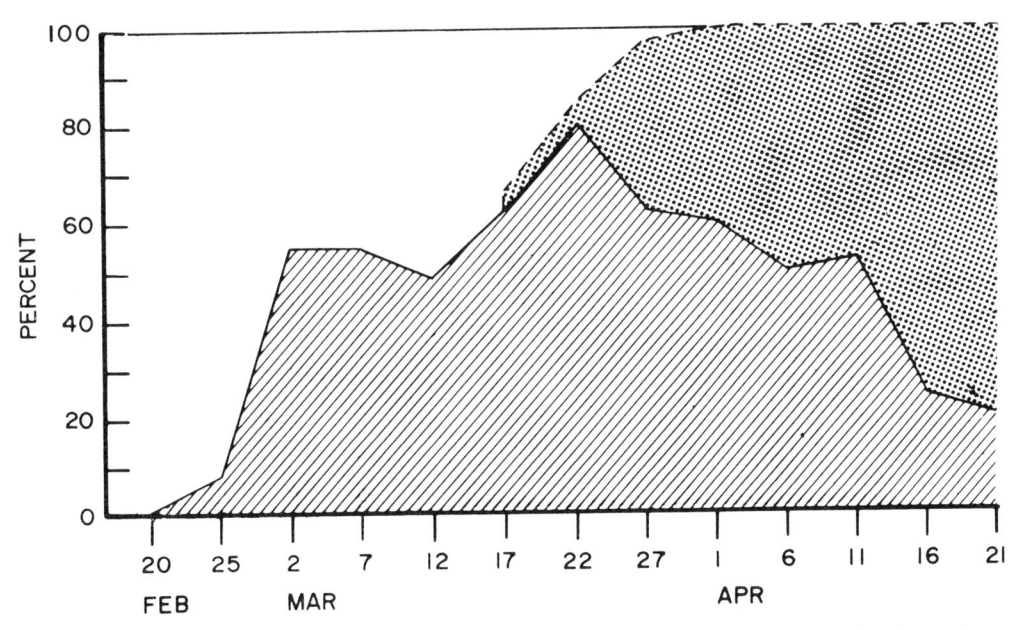

FIG. 19. Cumulative proportion of Bay-breasted Warblers in different molt classes in five day periods (plotted at end of period). The white portion indicates individuals that have not initiated any visible molt, lined areas indicate individuals that are molting, and stippled portions indicate individuals that have completed molt. Sample sizes (in order, by week) were 30, 20, 22, 42, 16, 44, 37, 15, 32, 15, 20, 12 (N = 305).

June, and produces more ripe fruit in April than March. This suggests that *Miconia* might play a critical role in providing nutrition for the contracted molt period in warblers on BCI. *Miconia* berries are easily procured. While some aggression occurs, particularly among Tennessee Warblers and between *Myiarchus tuberculifer* and other small birds; in general, the syndrome of superabundance characterizes the fruit crop of *Miconia* (McKey 1975; Howe and Estabrook 1977). Some trees produce literally hundreds of thousands of berries in a season. In addition, it is one of the smallest berries on BCI and is relatively easily swallowed by *Dendroica*.

To estimate the nutrition that warblers obtain by eating *Miconia*, I multiplied estimates of daily visitation rates of marked warblers by the average number of fruits consumed per visit. This estimate of the number of fruits eaten per day was multiplied by the nutritional content of *Miconia* berries. I took the product of this estimate and an arbitrary value of 0.8 for assimilation efficiency (see McDiarmid et al. 1977). See Appendix 1 for figures and calculations.

I estimate that warblers in the BCI clearing consumed 1.1 Kcal of *Miconia* berries each day during the peak of *Miconia* visitation. Based on a daily existence energy of 12 Kcal/day (formula from King 1974), I estimate that 9% of the normal daily energy needs are satisfied by *Miconia* berries. Molting can increase daily existence energy by as much as 20% (Payne 1972); *Miconia* may provide somewhat less than one twelfth the energy needs of a molting warbler. Since *Miconia* has practically no crude protein, it probably provides little more than an easily procured source of some of the daily energy requirements. The highly elevated protein demands must be satisfied, as suggested by Morton (1980), by insects. Still, Bay-breasted Warblers are highly attracted to *Miconia* trees; throughout much of March, few are found away from these trees. Either Bay-breasted Warblers are very close to not filling their energy demands, and this small increment of dependable food energy is necessary, or *Miconia* provides some critical nutrient. Warblers probably cease visiting *Miconia* as frequently when molt is completed because association with fruiting trees probably has considerable risk (Howe 1979). Warblers face particularly high risks since they often loaf and preen in and about fruiting trees.

OVERALL FORAGING SIMILARITIES AMONG FOLIAGE-GLEANING BIRDS ON BCI

Within the foliage-gleaning guild on BCI, major ecological groups can be distinguished on the basis of co-occurring traits. To cluster such groups, I have combined overlap values based on three principle variables that distinguish foliage-gleaning birds: foraging height distribution, foraging substrate, and degree of frugivory (Fig. 20). Other variables, such as foliage structure, leaf size, or crown cover, can be viewed as fine tuning variables that can be examined once the three principle variables are established.

I employed the most straightforward standard overlap index (Schoener 1968) since I am using it to depict similarity and not to infer competition. This method calls for the summation of the minimum value of the two species for each interval of a histogram. To combine the overlap values from individual overlaps, I take the

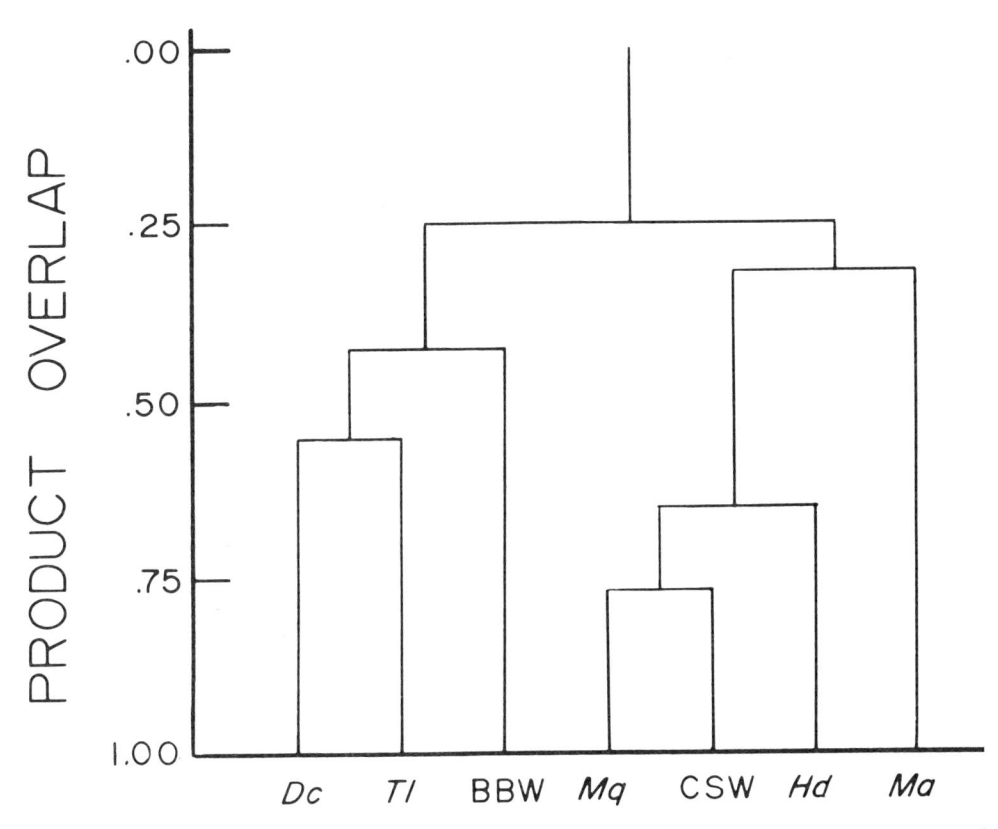

FIG. 20. Dendrogram based on the product overlap values between seven species of foliage-gleaning bird on BCI. The overall product overlap is based on simple overlaps (Schoener's formula) in foraging strata, foraging substrate, and degree of frugivory.

product; and species were clustered in a dendrogram on the basis of high product overlaps (Cody 1974). Use of the product assumes the independence of the three variables and gives low values (Cody 1974). While independence of foraging variables is probably rare in most situations, in this case, the assumption is probably not greatly violated. For one, the frequency of frugivory is independent of the insectivorous microhabitat. Secondly, the various foraging substrates (leaf tops, bottoms, twigs, etc.) occur more or less in similar relative abundance throughout the forest strata. The qualitative results would probably not change regardless of how the individual overlap values are combined; the correlation between summation and product overlaps was very high ($r = 0.95$) and the branching sequence of the dendrograms are identical.

From this analysis, it is clear that two distinct clusters are formed among the BCI foliage-gleaners. In addition, the two *Dendroica* occur in different subgroupings of foliage-gleaners. One cluster involves two tanagers, *Dacnis cayana* and *Tachyphonus luctuosus*, and the Bay-breasted Warbler. These species are omnivorous, forage frequently off the upper surface of leaves, and have similar foraging height distributions. In particular, these three species are common in the outer canopy. The other group includes the antwren, *Microrhopias*, *Hylophilus*, and Chestnut-sided Warbler. These three species occur at mid to high strata, rarely forage for fruit, and concentrate on hunting arthropods off the undersurface of leaves. *Myrmotherula axillaris* remains distinct from other foliage-gleaning birds primarily because of its unique foraging height distribution. *Hylophilus ochraceiceps*, common in mainland forests but not present on BCI, and the migrant *Wilsonia canadensis* would probably cluster with *Myrmotherula axillaris*.

BREEDING SEASON FORAGING BEHAVIOR

Bay-breasted and Chestnut-sided warblers showed most of the same foraging differences on the breeding grounds as on BCI, only they were more pronounced on the breeding grounds. Bay-breasted Warblers concentrate on gleaning insects from the upper surface of the foliage (sprays of spruce or fir needles); whereas, Chestnut-sided Warblers specialize on the lower surface of broad leaves (Table 30).

Correlated with the foraging substrate differences, Chestnut-sided Warblers tend to forage closer to the foliage over their head and farther from foliage on the same branch. This can be seen in Figures 21 and 22, which plot the frequency of warblers that have foliage within certain distances. The distributions of foliage above the warbler (Fig. 21) and on the same branch (Fig. 22) are significantly different between the two species (K.S. overhead foliage = 37, d.f. = 4, $p < .001$; K.S. same branch or level foliage = 59, $p < .001$).

The Chestnut-sided Warbler forages by shifting between branches frequently; the Bay-breasted Warbler hunts along branches (Table 31). The two species differ

Table 30. Proportional use of foraging substrates of breeding *Dendroica* in Maine

Species	N	Leaf Top[a]	Leaf Bottom	Twig	Air	Other
Yellow	115	.13	.72	.12	0	.05
Chestnut-sided	158	.11	.70	.13	.01	.04
Magnolia	81	.22	.58	.20	0	0
Palm	90	.78	.16	.02	.04	0
Cape May	26	.77	.08	.08	.08	.08
Bay-breasted	115	.65	.13	.17	.01	.04
Myrtle	43	.60	.16	.02	.14	0

a. For conifer foliage, "leaf top" and "leaf bottom" refer to the upper and lower surface of a spray of needles.

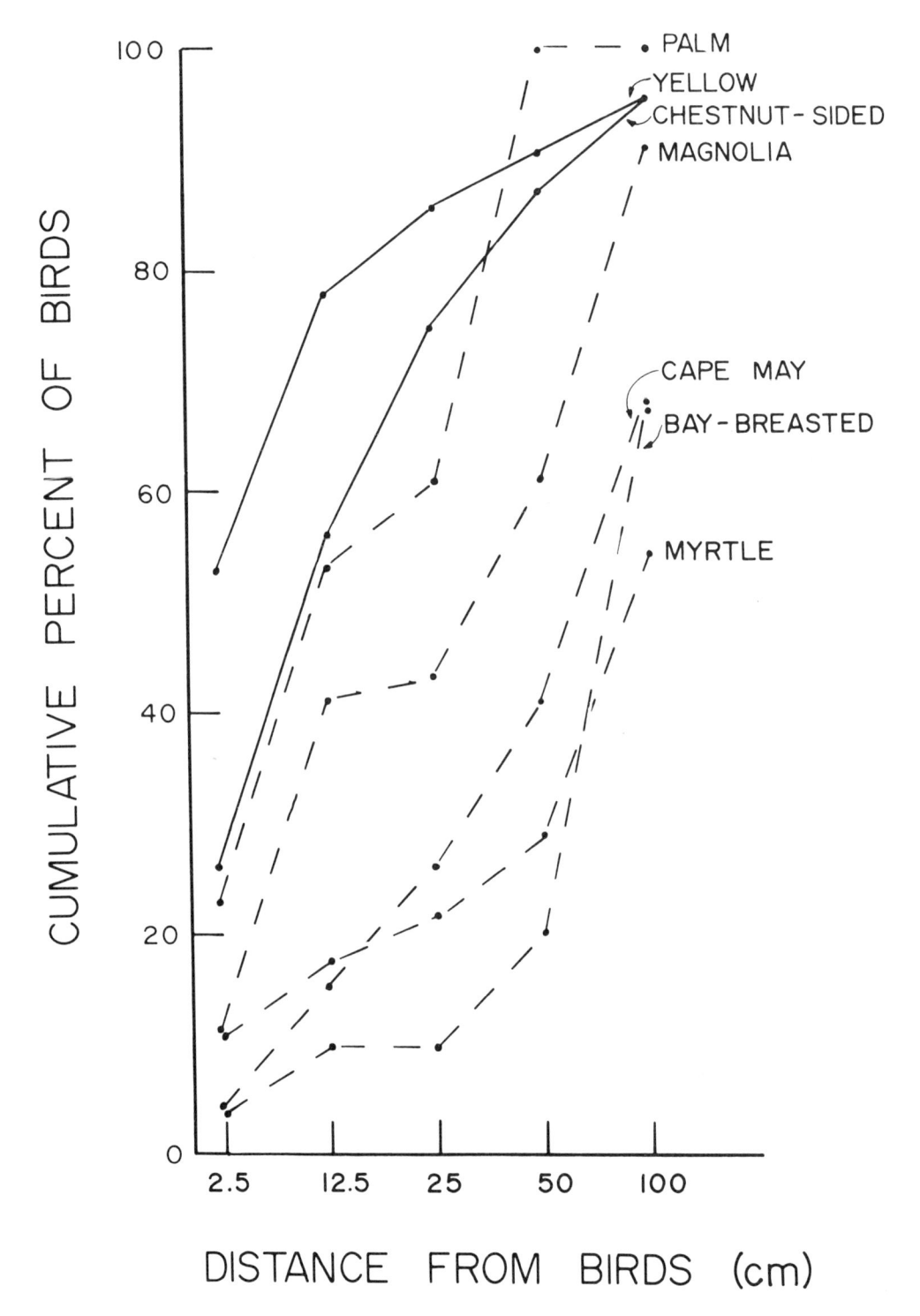

FIG. 21. Cumulative percent of foraging warblers with foliage within certain distances directly overhead. Each estimate was made after 30 seconds of observation. coniferous species are indicated by dashed and deciduous species by solid lines. Sample sizes are: Chestnut-sided (80), Yellow (40), Palm (15), Magnolia (47), Cape May (10), Bay-breasted (53), and Myrtle (27).

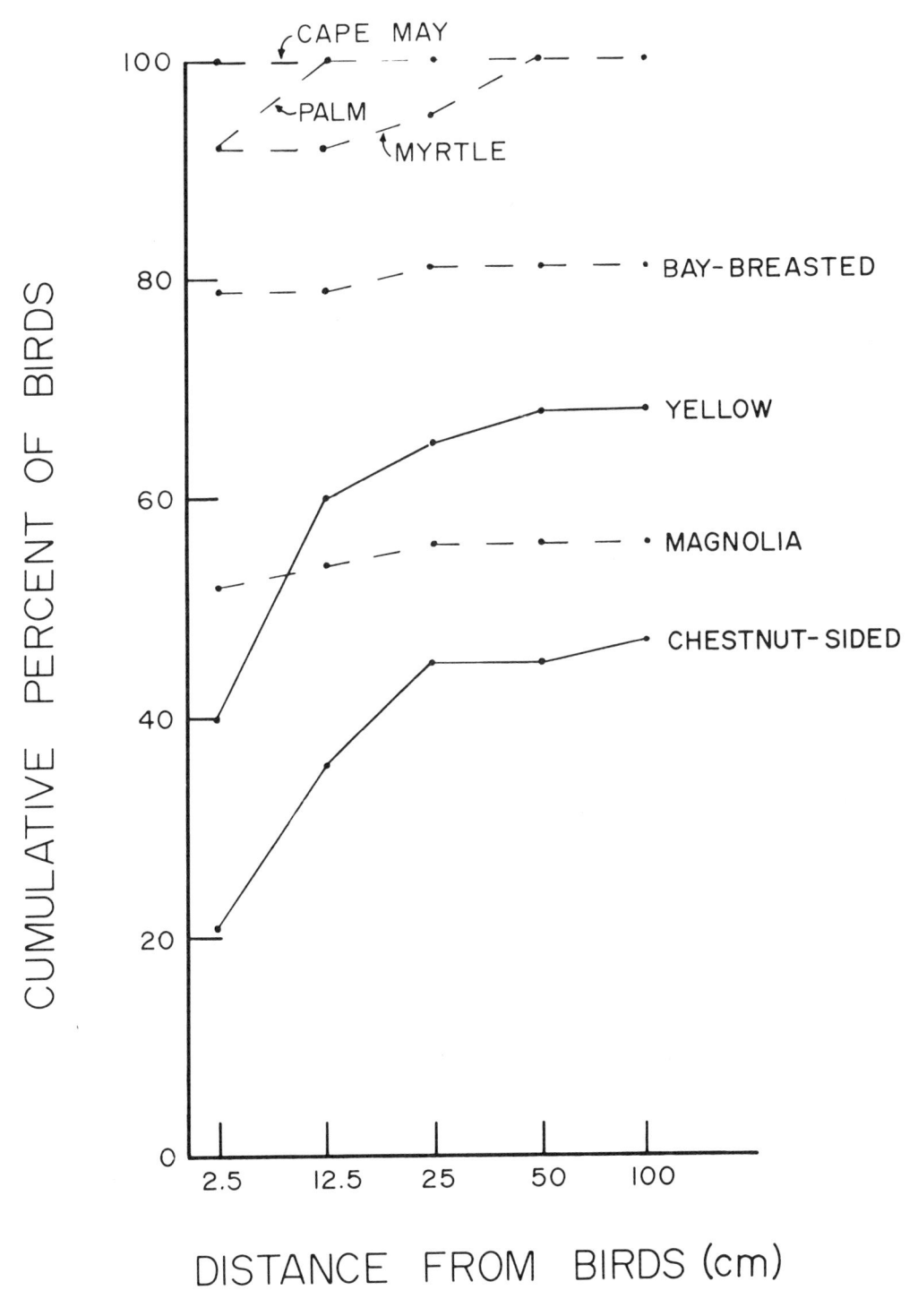

FIG. 22. Percentage of foraging warblers (Maine) within certain distances of foliage along the same branch (or the same horizontal plane but different branch). Each estimate was made after 30 seconds of observation. See Fig. 20 for sample sizes.

significantly when the creep:branch change ratio is analyzed by individual movement or distance travelled. Both MacArthur (1958) and Morse (1978) noted the tendency of Bay-breasted Warblers to creep slowly along major branch systems.

Chestnut-sided Warblers show much more active attack behavior than Bay-breasted Warblers on the breeding range. Less than two-thirds of the recorded attacks involved simple gleaning in the Chestnut-sided Warbler, as opposed to 95% in the Bay-breasted Warbler (Table 32). As in the BCI forest, Chestnut-sided Warblers frequently leaped and hovered.

In all aspects of foraging behavior that I quantified, Bay-breasted and Chestnut-sided warblers were more distinct on the breeding range than on the wintering range. In every case, this difference results primarily from the Bay-breasted Warbler shifting to become more similar to the Chestnut-sided Warbler on the wintering range. The most obvious example is the shift from coniferous to broad-leafed foliage by the Bay-breasted Warbler. The extreme specialization on upper surface foraging switches to a far more generalized use of leaf surfaces in the BCI forest (95% versus 45% upper). The Chestnut-sided Warbler, however, is remarkably similar between seasons in its substrate use. It forages slightly more often off twigs and petioles during the breeding season. Similarly, in searching movements, the Bay-breasted Warbler depends largely on creeping along branches on the breeding grounds, but shifts between branches relatively more often on BCI. The Bay-breasted Warbler moved 2.0 times along branches to every move between branches in Maine, but only 1.3 times along branches to each branch change on BCI. The Chestnut-sided Warbler, on the other hand, was very similar between seasons (0.44 breeding to 0.46 non-breeding). A similar pattern can be

Table 31. Breeding season foraging movement data for some northeastern *Dendroica* Warblers: creep/branch change by movement and distance

Species	N Males	N Females	Total Seconds	Movements	Distance
Yellow	18	8	3135	.39 (.04)[a]	.15 (.03)
Chestnut-sided	30	8	6905	.44 (.05)	.20 (.04)
Magnolia	20	8	3785	.45 (.06)	.19 (.02)
Palm	18[b]		2960	.43 (.08)	.16 (.02)
Yellow-rumped	6	7	2230	1.08 (.21)	.54 (.17)
Bay-breasted	24	11	5525	2.04 (.28)	.89 (.34)

a. Mean of all individuals with standard error in parentheses.
b. Sex not determined.

Table: 32. Proportion of foraging attack methods for breeding *Dendroica* in Maine

Species	N	Glean	Hover	Leap	Lunge	Sally
Yellow	115	.80	.09	.02	.08	.01
Chestnut-sided	158	.62	.17	.10	.07	.01
Magnolia	81	.61	.21	.07	.10	.02
Palm	90	.78	.07	.08	.01	.05
Cape May	26	.92	0	0	0	.08
Bay-breasted	115	.95	.03	0	.01	0
Yellow-rumped	43	.76	.12	0	.07	.03

found in the attack behavior (Table 26 & 32). The Bay-breasted Warbler gleaned 95% of the time in Maine as opposed to only 60% of the time on BCI. The Chestnut-sided Warbler, on the other hand, gleaned 62% in Maine and 40% on BCI.

By its specialization on the upper surface of foliage, the Bay-breasted Warbler is similar to several other coniferous forest *Dendroica* that I observed: Cape May, Myrtle, and Palm. The Chestnut-sided Warbler is similar to the deciduous scrub-breeding Yellow Warbler and the conifer and alder scrub-breeding Magnolia Warbler. Both of these species forage primarily off the undersurfaces of leaves.

In terms of the distribution of foliage around foraging warblers, the Bay-breasted Warbler is similar to Cape May and Myrtle warblers in having foliage close on the same branch, but relatively distant overhead (Figs. 21, 22). The Chestnut-sided Warbler is most similar to Yellow and Magnolia warblers in having foliage nearby overhead, but relatively far on the same branch (Figs. 21, 22). The Palm Warbler has foliage nearby overhead and on the same branch.

The Chestnut-sided warbler is also similar to Magnolia and Yellow warblers in its foraging movement pattern. Bay-breasted and Myrtle warblers both creep along branches as much or more than they shift between branches. My impression is that the Cape May Warbler also falls with the "creeping" warblers.

Chestnut-sided and Magnolia warblers depend more on active attack behavior than do other *Dendroica* I have observed. In this regard, the Yellow Warbler falls in with most coniferous warblers in using simple gleaning most of the time. The Bay-breasted Warbler, and to a lesser extent Myrtle, Cape May, and Palm warblers, glean to attack insects in conifer foliage (see summary Table 33).

Table 33. Summary of foraging ecology of some northeastern *Dendroica* (based on data collected in Maine in June-July 1980)

Species	Habitat	Foliage Surface	Attack	Movement	Foliage Overhead	Same Branch
Yellow	Deciduous scrub	under	glean	bc[a]	close	far
Chestnut-sided	Deciduous scrub	under	active[b]	bc	close	far
Magnolia	Coniferous scrub	under	active	bc	moderate	moderate
Palm	Coniferous swamp	upper	glean	bc	close	close
Yellow-rumped	Coniferous forest	upper	glean	creep	far	close
Cape May	Coniferous forest	upper	glean	creep	far	close
Bay-breasted	Coniferous forest	upper	glean	creep	far	close

a. bc = branch changer.
b. active refers to warblers that commonly employ leaping, hovering, or lunging to capture foliage arthropods.

DISCUSSION

Bay-breasted and Chestnut-sided warblers differ in nearly all aspects of their winter exploitation systems (Table 34). Bay-breasted Warblers show more seasonal fluctuation in density, are more intraspecifically gregarious, do not defend territories, and join mixed species flocks less frequently. In addition to these differences in social systems, the Bay-breasted Warbler is more generalized in its microhabitat preference, occurring equitably across forest strata and capturing insects off more substrate types. Further, the Bay-breasted Warbler is more omnivorous, switching more readily to eating small fruit.

Table 34. Summary of the exploitation systems of Bay-breasted and Chestnut-sided Warblers on BCI

	Chestnut-sided	Bay-breasted
Population fluctuation	little	pronounced seasonal decline
Group size	solitary	often in small groups
Mixed-species flocking	95%	60-80%
Common associates	canopy birds and antwrens	canopy birds, less with antwrens
Territoriality	small territories around antwren territories	rare, associated with a rich food source
Foraging strata	mid-level	diverse
Foraging substrate	leaf bottoms	diverse
Frugivory	5%	20-25%
Attack behavior	active attack common	active attack less common
Locomotion	branch changer	creeper

This dichotomy in winter exploitation systems can be seen in other temperate zone migrants in the Barro Colorado Island (BCI) forest. The Magnolia Warbler, while generally uncommon, was sufficiently abundant in 1978-1979 to observe and individually recognize a few birds regularly. They follow the Chestnut-sided Warbler pattern closely, defending small territories around antwren flocks. Rappole and Warner (1980) found Magnolia Warblers to defend small territories in lowland rain forest of Vera Cruz, Mexico. While I did not collect foraging data in any quantity, my impression is that the Magnolia Warbler is a largely insectivorous species favoring vine-tangles like *Microrhopias* (see Morton 1980; Willis 1980). Kentucky Warblers are restricted terrestrial insectivores and defend very small territories (Willis 1966; Karr 1976; Morton 1980; Rappole and Warner 1980; Gradwohl and Greenberg 1980). The insectivorous Canada Warbler occurs in antwren flocks as individuals or pairs that probably defend territories during the approximately six-week period that they pass through in spring migration (Greenberg and Gradwohl 1980a). The Tennessee Warbler, on the other hand, is highly gregarious, occurring in large groups reminiscent of the flocks of Bay-breasted Warblers that form in eastern Panama. They are highly omnivorous, visiting both fruiting and flowering trees. The Tennessee Warbler is frequently observed in flocks throughout Central America (Skutch 1957; Tramer 1974; Tramer and Kemp 1980; Morton 1980).

The universal rule that governs the winter exploitation systems of wood warblers and other neotropical migrants is that frugivorous or nectarivorous species are most likely to occur in flocks, but more restricted insectivorous species are nearly always solitary and defend territories. Other migrants that fit the omnivore syndrome include Red-eyed Vireo (*Vireo olivaceus*), Swainson Thrush (*Catharus ustulatus*), and Eastern Kingbird (*Tyrranus tyrranus*) (Morton 1971). Migrants that comprise the restricted insectivore group include Wood Thrush (*Hylocichla mustelina*), Great Crested Flycatcher (*Myiarchus crinitus*), Acadian Flycatcher (*Empidonax virescens*), and Yellow-throated Vireo (*Vireo flavifrons*).

The differences that are found between the similar Bay-breasted and Chestnut-sided warblers reflect a general dichotomy found among temperate migrants wintering in the Neotropics. A model for the evolution of diverse exploitation systems between members of *Dendroica* should provide general insight into the diversification of migrant strategies.

POSSIBLE FORAGING ADVANTAGES

An individual defending a small territory throughout the winter will reduce potential competition for food with conspecifics within that territory. Since the territories are defended throughout the winter, and warblers are primarily insectivorous for most of the winter, competition is reduced principally for arthropods found in the microhabitats searched by warblers. If the defended area is favorable, a territorial warbler may be able to survive on an insect diet throughout the winter. The disadvantage of this spacing behavior is that it limits the range covered by an individual warbler to a small defendable area. These warblers will be unable to use some areas that are favorable for short periods. In particular, fruiting trees which occur in low densities in a tropical forest will be an undependable resource for territorial warblers. On BCI, warblers visit only a few species of fruiting trees commonly (Greenberg 1981a). Since territories are established long before these preferred trees are fruiting, and territories are established around the territories of antwrens which are entirely insectivorous, territorial warblers probably cannot establish their range around fruiting trees except by chance. This creates the good possibility that a warbler will have little access to preferred fruiting trees throughout the winter. I have found some Chestnut-sided Warbler territories that appear to have no warbler-preferred fruiting trees.

Warblers that range over a large area may not gain exclusive access to any foraging areas. Large home ranges in dense tropical forest are probably indefensible by small birds, and thus alternative spacing systems are common (Willis 1966; Gradwohl and Greenberg 1980). The primary disadvantage of this spacing system would presumably be competition from conspecifics for use of favorable habitat to hunt arthropods. By wandering over a larger area, however, warblers might have a greater chance of locating sparsely distributed fruiting trees. The ability to aggregate from large areas (approximately 15 ha for Bay-breasted Warblers in this study) makes fruiting trees a dependable resource for nonterritorial warblers. The trees are almost never dominated or defended by individual warblers against conspecifics.

In this way, the social systems of Bay-breasted and Chestnut-sided warblers may reflect different degrees of dependence on fruit and arthropods throughout the winter. During periods of low foliage insect abundance, Bay-breasted Warblers may depend on alternative foods, whereas Chestnut-sided Warblers survive in local favorable refuges. Morton (1980) suggested that, in general, territorial species of migrants are restricted to more mesic sites to survive the dry season. Other species can move into more favorable areas or switch to alternative foods. I am suggesting a similar dichotomy between the two warblers, on a finer scale.

Why should there be two strategies among such closely related and morphologically similar species of migrants? The most reasonable explanation is that the Chestnut-sided Warbler exploits a richer foraging microhabitat. As a result, it is more buffered against seasonal fluctuations in food supply than the Bay-breasted Warbler. Several observations suggest that the Chestnut-sided Warbler is a more efficient foliage insectivore than the Bay-breasted Warbler. The Chestnut-sided Warbler is more specialized and more seasonally consistent in its foraging microhabitat. The Chestnut-sided Warbler concentrates on the richer foraging surface (Greenberg and Gradwohl 1980b). Finally, the Chestnut-sided Warbler is most similar in its foraging microhabitat to specialized resident insectivores such as *Hylophilis decurtatus* and *Microrhopias*; whereas, the Bay-breasted Warbler is similar to some resident omnivorous species, which are also less dependent upon foliage insects during the dry season. Morton (1980) found that Bay-breasted Warblers, but not Chestnut-sided Warblers, took smaller prey during the dry season, an observation that suggests that their insectivorous foraging efficiency was reduced.

THE RELATIONSHIP BETWEEN SOCIAL BEHAVIOR AND PREDATION

Factors other than foraging efficiency could account for the divergent social systems of Bay-breasted and Chestnut-sided warblers. Predation, for example, has often been implicated as important in selecting for divergent spacing behavior. While predation pressure may be high in tropical forests, no specific predator avoidance strategies are consistent with Bay-breasted Warblers occurring in small groups and Chestnut-sided Warblers defending small territories.

Single species flocking may or may not be important in reducing predation. Page and Whitacre (1975) showed that predation pressure was higher for sandpipers in smaller groups. Myers (1980; unpubl.), and Caraco et al. (1980) found that birds often abandon territories in the presence of aerial predators. Flocking may also allow birds to spend less time searching for potential predators and more time foraging (Buskirk 1976; Powell 1974; Pulliam 1973; Willis 1972).

On the other hand, flocks can be conspicuous and may attract predators, thereby increasing the predation rate. This has been suggested to be important for birds visiting fruiting trees in predator-rich areas (Howe 1979). While the evidence is poor for adult birds, some data suggests that bird nests fare better against predation if they are dispersed and not clumped (Tinbergen et al. 1967).

The difference in single species gregariousness in *Dendroica* is probably not determined by predation. It should be remembered that while I have emphasized the differences in the distribution of the two species in the BCI forest, they actually show a high degree of co-occurrence. They overlap greatly in foraging strata and occur frequently in the same mixed species flocks. Distribution along census routes indicates no special habitat preference within the BCI forest. Because of this high degree of co-occurrence, the two species probably experience the same predator environment.

While they may occur in the same predator environment, they could experience this environment differently because of different foraging strategies. The Bay-breasted Warbler is a more extensive forager since it peers in all directions, rather than primarily in one direction, as does the Chestnut-sided Warbler. Bay-breasted Warblers could gain security from predation by foraging with conspecifics that are also peering in a variety of directions. Willis (1972) proposed that *Myrmotherula axillaris* occurs in "clans" for similar reasons. The plausibility of this argument for warblers is severely reduced since I never detected any sort of alarm notes used by warblers in the presence of potential predators or humans. Also, if their foraging behavior allows them to be more vigilant to predators, I would expect warbler flocks to form outside of mixed species flocks. In fact, almost all Bay-breasted Warblers out of mixed species flocks were solitary.

The Chestnut-sided Warbler, however, probably gains little in terms of reduced predation by driving conspecifics out of their territories. Chestnut-sided Warblers almost invariably forage in mixed species flocks; unless predators somehow specialize on warblers, the exclusion of one conspecific is a negligible reduction in local bird density.

MIXED SPECIES FLOCKING

The differences in frequency of occurrence at mixed species flocks is not great between the two species. The observed minor difference probably reflects the difference in spacing behavior of the two species. The territorial system of the Chestnut-sided Warbler is probably, in part, a mechanism for insuring a dependable mixed species flock association. *Microrhopias*, *Myrmotherula fulviventris*, and the Chestnut-sided Warbler probably do not defend the same size territory because of identical energy demands (Munn and Terborgh 1979). The precision of the co-defended territory system is probably a result of the consistently high fidelity of the birds at mixed flocks.

Bay-breasted Warblers rarely showed this sort of fidelity to one mixed species flock system. Individuals presumably must move between flocks. This alone may account for the 15-20% lower frequency of occurrence of Bay-breasted Warblers at mixed species flocks.

Bay-breasted Warblers are less strongly associated with the antwren flock nucleus; they more often occur with the canopy species *Tachyphonus luctuosus* and *Hylophilus*. Observation of a loose group of Bay-breasted Warblers from the BCI canopy tower indicated that these loose associations remain in a particular location throughout the winter and follow flocks of varied composition that moved through this area. This contrasts with the flock following strategy of the Chestnut-sided Warbler, which follows one group of birds persistently.

Despite differences in mixed flock following behavior, the two species show similarity in the kinds of flocks followed. Both species join flocks of small insectivorous birds and the advantages accrued by following these flocks are probably similar. The most important advantage is probably the avoidance of predation. In other words, while the difference in intraspecific gregariousness cannot be related to differences in predation avoidance, the similarity in interspecific flocking is probably a similar response to potentially high predation.

The idea that warblers join flocks primarily to locate unfamiliar food sources seems unlikely. The most omnivorous species are seldom joined in mixed species flocks; flocks of *Tangara*, *Cyanerpes*, and *Heterospingus* move too rapidly for the methodical warblers to follow. The most frugivorous of the common warbler associates, *Tachyphonus luctuosus* and *Myiarchus tuberculifer*, are still predominantly insectivorous, except in the late dry season. I rarely observed warblers follow flocks into or out of fruiting trees. Warblers usually remain near a fruiting tree between feeding bouts; whereas, resident species enter and leave the vicinity of the tree. With one of the preferred species, *Lindackeria laurina*, resident species rarely visited the tree. The dependence of migrants on residents for locating food plants may have been overstated by previous authors (Leck 1972).

It is still possible that migrants learn about the distribution of insects by joining mixed species flocks. This seems unlikely for the Chestnut-sided Warbler, because this species shows such extreme specialization in its microhabitat use. Foliage insects show no patchiness in their distribution beyond the patchiness found in foliage density. Bay-breasted Warblers monitor a more varied regime of microhabitats; it is conceivable that they could learn about the productivity of different foraging sites by watching individuals of other species such as was reported for species of *Parus* (Krebs 1973). The association between Bay-breasted Warblers and other species within a flock is rather loose. Most Bay-breasted Warblers are not found foraging within 5 m of another bird. Visual contact is improbable at this distance.

Both species of warbler face a regime of unfamiliar predators. Whether predation on adult birds is more or less intense in tropical forests has yet to be determined. The diversity of types of potential predators is unarguably greater in tropical forests. The complexity of the physical environment further increases the unfamiliarity of the predator regime. The warblers appear to have no distinct predator alarm system and were not observed to actively mob snakes, hawks, or humans, as did certain residents (antshrikes, antwrens, and greenlets). The Chestnut-sided Warbler seems to be particularly vulnerable since it directs its search effort towards one microhabitat (leaf undersurface) and peers in one direction (up). While I have little direct evidence that the joining of flocks reduces predation on wintering warblers, it is easy at least to envision how association with species, such as *Microrhopias* with well developed predator alarm systems, might be advantageous.

PROBABLE BREEDING SEASON INFLUENCE ON WINTER EXPLOITATION SYSTEMS

Conditions on the breeding grounds may be critical in determining the divergent winter exploitation systems. The structure of the foliage and the distribution of arthropods can shape morphological and behavioral foraging adaptations, which in turn can tip the balance towards a more conservative or opportunistic strategy. Three features of the biology of Bay-breasted and Chestnut-sided warblers suggest that adaptation to breeding season conditions is probably the driving force in the diversification of winter behavior: body size, leaf surface preference, and search behavior. I am not suggesting these three aspects are themselves independent, merely that they are sufficiently disparate to indicate how thoroughly breeding season factors affect warbler adaptations.

Body Size. Bay-breasted and Chestnut-sided warblers differ greatly in body size. In fact, the Bay-breasted Warbler averages approximately 25% heavier. While the Chestnut-sided Warbler is similar in size to the local resident foliage-gleaning specialists (i.e., those species that subsist nearly totally on arthropods), the Bay-breasted Warbler is approaching the small omnivorous tanagers in body size (Table 35). A 25% increase in body size could profoundly affect the agility of a small active insectivorous bird.

Body size is strongly related to the breeding habitat occupied by *Dendroica* (Greenberg 1979). The largest species are those restricted to coniferous vegetation. The functional significance of this relationship has been discussed (Greenberg 1979) and will be pursued below. The relationship itself, however, suggests the importance of breeding season conditions in shaping winter behavior. Resident species and races, such as the Pine Warbler (*D. pinus*) and Central American populations of the Yellow-rumped Warbler (*D. coronata goldmanii*), share their large body size with species that breed in conifers but migrate into

Table 35. Body weight of active foliage-gleaning birds in a lowland Panamanian forest, with species divided into major foraging groups

Group 1: Undersurface foragers; mid-level, restricted insectivores	Wt[a]	Group 2: Upper surface foragers or surface generalists; upper level, omnivores
Mymotherula brachyura	7 g	
M. axillaris	8	
Microrhopias quixensis	8	
Hylophilus decurtatus	9	
Chestnut-sided Warbler	9	
Hylophilus ochraceiceps	10	
	11.5	Bay-breasted Warbler
	12	*Dacnis cayana*
	13-14	*Tachyphonus luctuosus*
	40	*Heterospingus rubrifrons*

a. Weights from banding data, museum skins from the Louisiana State University or Karr 1971.

broad-leafed habitats. This suggests that the occupation of conifer vegetation, and not any wintering ground factor, is critical in selecting for large body size.

Leaf Surface Preference. The Chestnut-sided Warbler is more restricted to foraging off the undersurfaces of leaves than is the Bay-breasted Warbler. In this regard, the Chestnut-sided warbler is typical of Panamanian forest birds that depend upon foliage arthropods throughout the year. This is also typical of foliage-gleaning birds in broad-leafed forests of eastern North America (Holmes and Robinson unpubl.).

A strong preference for foraging on leaf undersurfaces probably occurs for two reasons. The arthropod fauna is far richer on this substrate than on leaf upper surfaces, particularly when highly mobile prey such as adult Diptera are not considered (Greenberg and Gradwohl 1980b). It is also probably easier to view a large number of leaf undersurfaces. The view of leaf upper surfaces on branches below a foraging bird will probably be obscured by the vegetation on the branch on which the bird is perched. In Panamanian forests, species that commonly forage off the upper surfaces of foliage are generally omnivorous, and are thus less dependent upon foliage insects during the dry season (Greenberg and Gradwohl 1980b). On the other hand, species may have specialized search or attack behavior which makes leaf upper surface foraging more advantageous. *Tachyphonus*, for example, jumps down rapidly from branch tips, to the exposed surfaces of foliage below; *Dacnis* probes into areas of leaf damage from leaf petioles.

The frequent use of upper leaf surfaces by the Bay-breasted Warbler remains a puzzle since it displays no such distinctive tactics for leaf top foraging. Observation of the Bay-breasted Warbler on the breeding grounds places the winter foraging behavior in a new context. When foraging along spruce or fir foliage, Bay-breasted Warblers are truly specialized on foraging off the upper surface of the foliage.

Leaf upper surface foraging is common among conifer-dwelling *Dendroica* and other parulids. I have shown that Myrtle, Cape May, Palm, and Bay-breasted Warblers all forage primarily off the upper surface of conifer foliage; the Tennessee Warbler is a "leaf top" forager as well in spruce-fir forest. Partridge (1976) suggested that a conifer foraging parid differs from a broad-leafed foraging parid by foraging off the upper surface of foliage. While arthropods are more common on the lower surface of spruce-fir foliage (unpubl. data), most arthropods can be attacked by probing into the needles from above; needles do not form a protective sheet as do leaves. In addition, caterpillars (particularly spruce budworms) generally insinuate themselves within the needles and need to be extracted. This can be accomplished easily by pulling at foliage on the same branch.

The structure of the foliage also favors leaf top foraging in large coniferous trees. In spruce or fir, the foliage is tightly clustered around branches, upon which warblers can perch and move. The lack of an obvious analog of the leaf petiole aids easy exploitation of foliage on the same branch system. The pagoda-shaped structure of large spruce or fir trees places foliage in sheets that are widely spaced and prevent easy attack from other branches. This renders large portions of the foliage in spruce-fir forest accessible only to leaf top foragers that forage along the branch systems.

In view of the Bay-breasted Warbler's nearly complete restriction to leaf top foraging during the breeding season, its use of upper leaf surfaces in Panamanian forests seems less puzzling. Bay-breasted Warblers are probably restricted from completely switching to a foraging mode appropriate for broad-leafed insectivory by morphological and behavioral adaptations to foliage experienced on the breeding grounds. The Chestnut-sided Warbler, on the other hand, forages off the undersurface of broad leaves on the breeding grounds. Recall that the Bay-breasted Warbler consistently showed the greatest modification in foraging behavior between breeding and winter seasons (p. 82).

Searching Behavior. The Chestnut-sided Warbler hops rapidly from branch to branch, peering upward. The Bay-breasted Warbler creeps methodically along single branches, slowly moving its head from side to side. Motion along a single branch system is rare among resident foliage insectivores, such as *Myrmotherula axillaris*, *Microropias*, and *Hylophilus*; it is characteristic of *Tachyphonus*.

Creeping along branches does not seem to make as much sense, a priori, as changing branches as a method of searching broad-leafed vegetation. In the forest understory, foliage tends to be distributed in broad horizontal sprays. These sheets provide a display of leaf surfaces. To maximize the number of leaf surfaces viewed per unit time or distance moved, a foraging bird should shift between branches more than moving along branches. Movements between branches bring new planes of foliage into view; whereas, movements along branches slightly shift the view of the same foliage.

This argument assumes that the foraging bird is searching a sphere of foliage that includes leaf surfaces on branches above it. A relatively short attack distance, such as is found in the Bay-breasted Warbler, may restrict it to searching leaves on the branch on which it is perched. Because of this, the advantages of shifting branches may be reduced for the Bay-breasted Warbler.

Once again, in the context of breeding range foliage structure, the short attack distance and creeping locomotion can be better understood. Bay-breasted Warblers I observed foraging in spruce-fir forest had an exaggerated creeping locomotion when compared to my observations in Panama. Bay-breasted Warblers forage in the portions of large conifers where branches tend to be widely separated (this study; MacArthur 1958; Morse 1978). They were generally found at least one meter from foliage overhead. Because of the inaccessibility of foliage in adjacent branch systems, Bay-breasted Warblers commonly move outward along the boughs of large trees. This creeping motion is characteristic of coniferous breeding *Dendroica* such as Myrtle (when foliage-gleaning and not sallying for aerial insects), Cape May (this study) and Pine warblers (Bent 1953). Creeping along branches is not a universal characteristic of coniferous breeding warblers. Palm and Magnolia warblers are frequent hoppers (this study), and MacArthur found that Black-throated Green Warblers are branch changers as well. Magnolia and Black-throated Green warblers will be discussed more fully below. Palm Warblers forage in small adult conifers at the edge of sphagnum bogs. These 5-20 foot larches and black spruce have mature pagoda-like growth form, but have short narrowly spaced branches due to their small size. While Palm Warblers search the upper surface of the branch on which they are perched, they do so by moving frequently between the small branches.

THE EVOLUTION OF WINTER EXPLOITATION SYSTEMS IN DENDROICA

Earlier, I discussed the intercorrelation among such disparate aspects of *Dendroica* biology as body size, breeding habitat, and winter social systems (Greenberg 1979). To this we can add one more correlate: the surface of the foliage exploited on the breeding grounds. Of 10 species of northeastern *Dendroica*, for which I have data or for which equivalent data are available, the small bodied warblers (8-9 g) are the leaf bottom specialists; whereas, the large bodied warblers (10-12 g) forage off the upper surface of foliage (see Table 36). In fact, the foliage surface hunted by warblers is a powerful predictor of body size and winter social behavior. The most glaring exceptions to the breeding habitat body size correlation explored in Greenberg (1979), i.e., Black-throated Green and Magnolia warblers, are similar to other small bodied warblers on the basis of foliage surface use.

The functional relationship between body size and leaf surface preference is straightforward. Underleaf foragers are generally more agile, employing leaping attack motions to capture or flush arthropods and rapid branch changes to search foliage. Leaf top foragers are most often simple probers or gleaners. Why

Table 36. Leaf surface preference in some Northeastern *Dendroica* Warblers

Species of Warbler	Weight	Habitat[d]	Percentage of foraging on leaf undersurface[a]
Yellow	9 g	Deciduous	85
Chestnut-sided	9	Deciduous	88
Black-throated Green	9	Coniferous	mostly undersides[b]
		Deciduous	65[c]
Blackburnian	10	Deciduous	55[c]
Black-throated Blue	8	Deciduous	85[c]
Palm	11	Coniferous	19
Bay-breasted	12	Coniferous	17
Cape May	10	Coniferous	9
Yellow-rumped	12	Coniferous	21
Magnolia	8	Coniferous	73

a. Percent of foliage foraging motions.
b. MacArthur 1958.
c. R.T. Holmes pers. comm.
d. Habitat of study.

Magnolia and Black-throated Green warblers forage in a manner more typical of broad-leafed *Dendroica* is also readily understood. The Magnolia Warbler forages in very dense conifer shrubbery (as well as alder thickets). The interbranch distances are small and foliage is easily accessible overhead. Foliage is nearly as close as it is for broad-leafed scrub *Dendroica* (Fig. 21). With small potential attack distances, it becomes more potentially profitable to attack the richer underleaf surface. The Black-throated Green Warbler also forages in areas of high foliage density (Morse 1971, 1976).

The following scenario relates breeding ground foraging to winter social systems (Table 37). In broad-leafed or dense conifer foliage, warblers attack the under surface of the vegetation, which requires greater agility and smaller body size. Upon migrating into regions with only broad-leafed vegetation, these species are able to efficiently attack leaf undersurfaces throughout the winter. In lower density conifer foliage, warblers forage by picking and probing the upper surface of nearby foliage; neither agility nor small body size are favored. Upon migrating into areas with only broad-leafed vegetation, they are inefficient at attacking foliage insects. During periods of low arthropod abundance, these species switch to nonfoliage insects (aerial, ground, or bark), fruit, or nectar. The species that concentrate on foliage insects throughout the year defend small patches of good habitat. The conifer species that switch to alternative food types range over a larger area to locate insect concentrations or fruiting and flowering trees.

WARBLERS AS AN ECOLOGICAL UNIT IN THE BCI FOREST

The fact that the two *Dendroica* cluster with different species of resident foliage gleaners (Fig. 20) and that the exploitation systems are so dramatically different suggests that quite different resources are being used. If no consistent and easily described strategy can be assigned to two such similar migrant species, it is unlikely that a general unifying strategy can be defined for migrants in Panamanian forests. In fact, among the foliage-gleaning species, the Chestnut-sided Warbler is in most ways the most specialized and the Bay-breasted Warbler is both generalized and plastic in its foraging behavior. These two warbler species reflect part of the range of foraging strategies present among small tropical forest foliage-gleaning birds.

These two congeneric migrants cluster into distinct ecological strategies within a tropical avifauna, and this casts some doubt on the validity of looking for

Table 37. The possible evolutionary basis of divergent winter exploitation systems in *Dendroica*

Breeding foliage structure	Broad-leafed or dense conifer	Conifer
Leaf surface exploited	Under surface	Upper surface
Agility; attack method	Agility high; leaping common	Agility low; leaping uncommon
Body Size	Small body (< 10 g)	Large body (> 10 g)
Proficiency at exploiting broad-leaf insects in winter	Good	Poor
Dependence on alternate foods	Low	High
Winter social system	Territorial	Nonterritorial
Examples:	Chestnut-sided	Bay-breasted
	Yellow	Palm
	Magnolia	Yellow-rumped
	Black-throated Blue	Cape May
	Black-throated Green	Blackpoll (?)

structure within migrant species assemblages in themselves. Bay-breasted and Chestnut-sided warblers show largely allopatric distributions, which might be attributed to their mutual competition in sympatry. However, closer examination in sympatry suggests that each species is more likely to experience competition with resident insectivores. In addition, the differences in social behavior found in sympatry are, if anything, exaggerated in allopatry, not in sympatry (pp. 30, 34). If differences in social systems reflect the nature of food exploited, then it is likely that differences in foraging strategy are found throughout the species' ranges, not just in sympatry. On the other hand, competition with resident species cannot easily account for the restricted winter ranges of Bay-breasted and Chestnut-sided warblers. The same complement of small, specialized, foliage-gleaning birds is found in Costa Rica and Panama (Ridgely 1976). More species of small omnivorous foliage gleaners occur in eastern Panama and Colombia, where Bay-breasted Warblers are most common. *Hemithraupis* may be the closest ecological analog to the Bay-breasted Warbler, and it is not found in the Canal Area.

The Bay-breasted Warbler shows some fundamental differences from other Panamanian forest birds. It is extremely generalized in its foraging substrates, foraging height distribution, and habitat preference. Seasonal shifts in foraging microhabitat are more pronounced than in other foliage gleaners. The fluid social system of Bay-breasted Warblers allow local densities to increase at local insect concentrations and fruiting trees. The high densities in which Bay-breasted Warblers are found, especially in eastern Panama, suggest that its behavioral plasticity forms the basis of an extremely successful exploitation system for lowland tropical forests.

Clearly, it is not the only successful strategy for wintering in the tropics. The Chestnut-sided Warbler is relatively undistinguished from other foliage-gleaning birds. In the BCI forest, it is rather restricted in its microhabitat distribution and its densities are low to moderate. Because of its rigid territorial spacing system, individuals are scattered throughout the forest. The Chestnut-sided Warbler displays, however, a wide habitat distribution when compared to other forest foliage gleaning birds, such as *Hylophilus decurtatus* and *Microrhopias*. Unlike these species, and similar to the Bay-breasted Warbler, *Tachyphonus luctuosus*, and *Dacnis*, the Chestnut-sided Warbler can be found in a wide variety of second-growth and dry forest habitats.

CONCLUDING REMARKS

I have gained several general insights from this detailed study of two tropical wintering migrant warblers.

To understand the significance of a morphological or behavioral characteristic of a species, it is necessary to take a holistic view of its activities across seasons. While it is probably incorrect to assert the preeminence of the activities of a single season in shaping adaptations (Rappole and Warner 1980), some aspects of the ecology of a species can best be understood in the context of conditions faced in a particular season (Fretwell 1972).

Close relationship, similarity in overall morphology, or similarity in migratory behavior do not confer ecological similarity upon species of birds. For most considerations, a category such as "migrant warbler" is meaningless as an ecological class.

Differences in resource use between some species may not reflect differences in morphology or locomotion so much as a difference in perception. Many of the differences between Bay-breasted and Chestnut-sided warblers may result from how individuals of the species perceive resource availability in a tropical forest, not just on a day-to-day basis, but over entire winters. Foraging studies should avoid undue emphasis on a deterministic relationship between morphology and foraging behavior and concentrate on differences in perception, exploratory behavior, learning abilities, and other factors that determine foraging plasticity.

Appendix

Calculations for the Estimate of Energy Obtained from *Miconia argentea* Berries by *Dendroica* in the BCI Clearing

$\bar{X}$ visits/hr = 0.7 (0.14 s.e.), based on five marked Bay-breasted and two marked Chestnut-sided warblers observed over 15 hr. in two-hour periods divided between morning and afternoon, early and late fruiting period.

$\bar{X}$ fruits eaten/visit = 6 (20 visits)

Grams of Miconia berries eaten/day = 12 hr/day × 0.7 visits/hr × 0.02 g (dry wt)/berry = 1 g/day

Since seeds comprise 15-20% of the total dry weight and have over twice as much nitrogen as the total berry, I conclude that essentially all of the crude protein is in the seeds. Since the seeds have less than 0.1% nonstructural carbohydrates and lipids, I assume all of the fat and carbohydrates are in the pulp. Warblers ate approximately 60% unripe and 40% ripe fruit; I use a low estimate of nonstructural carbohydrates for my estimate of calories.

Kcal/g fruit = 0.25 carbohydrates/g fruit × 4.2 Kcal/g carbohydrates + 02. g lipids/g fruit × 9.2 Kcal/g lipids = 1.25 Kcal/g fruit Kcal/day = 1.25 Kcal/g fruit × 1 g fruit/day × 0.8 assimilation = 1 Kcal.

Literature Cited

Bennett, C. F.
    1968. Human influences on the zoogeography of Panama. Ibero-American, 51:1-112.

Bennett, S. E.
    1980. Interspecific competition and the niche of the American Redstart (*Setophaga ruticilla*) in wintering and breeding communities. Pp. 319-337 in A. Keast and E. S. Morton, eds. Migrant birds in the Neotropics: ecology, behavior, distribution, and conservation. Smithsonian Inst. Press., Washington, D.C.

Bent, A. C.
    1953. Life history of North American wood warblers. United States National Museum Bulletin No. 303.

Bond, J.
    1957. North American warblers in the West Indies. Pp. 257-263, in L. Griscom and A. Sprunt, eds. The warblers of North America. Devin-Adair, New York.

Buskirk, W. H.
    1976. Social systems in a tropical forest avifauna. Amer. Nat., 110:292-310.

Caraco, T. S., S. Martindale, and H. R. Pulliam
    1980. Avian flocking in the presence of a predator. Nature, 285:400-401.

Chapman, F. M.
    1938. Life in an air castle. Appleton Co., New York.

Chipley, R. M.
    1980. Nonbreeding ecology of the Blackburnian Warbler. Pp. 309-319, in A. Keast and E. S. Morton, eds. Migrant birds in the neotropics: ecology, behavior, distribution, and conservation. Smithsonian Inst. Press, Washington, D.C.

Cody, M. L.
    1974. Competition and the structure of bird communities. Monogr. in Pop. Biol., Princeton University Press, Princeton, New Jersey.

Cox, G. W.
    1968. The role of competition in the evolution of migration. Evol., 22:180-189.

Croat, T. B.
    1978. Flora of Barro Colorado Island. Stanford Univ. Press, Stanford, Calif.

Crook, J. H.
    1965. The adaptive significance of avian social organizations: Symposium Zool. Soc., London, 14:181-218.

Dwight, J. R.
    1900. Plumages and moults in passerine birds. Annals N. Y. Acad. Sci., 3:73-360.

Eaton, S. W.
    1953. Wood Warblers wintering in Cuba. Wilson Bull., 65:169-174.

Literature Cited

Eisenmann, E.
- 1957. Wood warblers in Panama. Pp. 286-298 in L. Griscom and A. Sprunt, eds. The warblers of North America. Devin-Adair, New York.

Erskine, A.
- 1977. Birds in boreal Canada: communities, densities, and adaptations. Can. Wild. Serv. Rep. Ser. No. 4.

Ficken, M. S. and R. W. Ficken
- 1963. The comparative ethology of the wood warblers: a review. Living Bird, 1:103-121.

Foster, R. B.
- 1973. Seasonality of fruit production and seed fall in a tropical forest. Unpublished Ph.D dissertation. Duke University, Durham, N. C.

Fretwell, S.
- 1972. Populations in a seasonal environment. Monogr. in Pop. Biol. Princeton University Press, Princeton, N. J.
- 1980. Evolution of migration in relation to factors regulating bird numbers. Pp. 517-529 in A. Keast and E. S. Morton, eds. Migrant birds in the Neotropics: ecology, behavior, distribution, and conservation. Smithsonian Inst. Press, Washington, D.C.

Gradwohl, J. and R. Greenberg
- 1980. The formation of antwren flocks on Barro Colorado Island, Panama. Auk, 97:385-396.
- 1983. The breeding season of antwrens on Barro Colorado Island, Panama. Pp. 345-351 in E. G. Leigh, ed. Seasonal rhythms in a tropical forest. Smithsonian Inst. Press, Washington, D.C.

Greenberg, R.
- 1979. Body size, breeding habitat, and winter exploitation systems in *Dendroica*. Auk, 96:756-766.
- 1980. Demographic aspects of long-distance migration in birds. Pp. 493-505 in A. Keast and E. S. Morton, eds. Migrant birds in the Neotropics: ecology, behavior, distribution, and conservation. Smithsonian Inst. Press, Washington, D.C.
- 1981a. The frugivorous behavior of some tropical forest wood warblers. Biotropica, 13:215-223
- 1981b. Dissimilar bill morphology in tropical versus temperate forest foliage-gleaning birds. Oecologia, 49:143-147.
- 1981c. The abundance and seasonality of forest canopy birds on Barro Colorado Island, Panama. Biotropica, 13:241-251.

Greenberg, R. and J. Gradwohl
- 1980a. Observations of paired Canada warblers, *Wilsonia canadensis*, during migration in Panama. Ibis, 106:86-89.
- 1980b. Leaf surface specialization in arthopods and birds of a Panamanian forest. Oecologia, 46: 115-124.

Hartshorne, G.
- 1978. Tree falls and tropical forest dynamics. Pp. 617-639, in P. B. Tomlinson and M. H. Zimmermann, eds. Tropical trees as living systems. Cambridge Univ. Press, Cambridge, England.

Hespenheide, H. A.
- 1980. Bird community structure in two Panamanian forests. Pp. 227-239, in A. Keast and E. S. Morton, eds. Migrant birds in the Neotropics: ecology, behavior, distribution, and conservation. Smithsonian Inst. Press, Washington, D.C.

Literature Cited

Holderidge, L. R.
   1967. Life zone ecology. Tropical Science Center, San Jose, Costa Rica.

Holmes, R. T., R. E. Bonney, and S. W. Pacala
   1979. Guild structure of the Hubbard Brook bird community: a multivariate approach. Ecology, 60:512-520.

Holmes, R. T. and S. K. Robinson.
   1981. Tree species preference of foraging insectivorous birds in a northern hardwood forest. Oecologia, 48:31-35.

Howe, H. F.
   1979. Fear and frugivory. Amer. Nat., 114:925-931.

Howe, H. F. and G. Estabrook
   1977. On intraspecific competition for avian dispersers in tropical trees. Amer. Nat., 111:817-832.

Jones, M. S.
   1980. The spruce-budworm disaster. Amer. Forest, 6:17-21.

Jones, S. E.
   1977. Coexistence in mixed species antwren flocks. Oikos, 29:366-375.

Karr, J. R.
   1971. Structure of avian communities in selected Panama and Illinois habitats. Ecol. Monogr., 44:207-227.
   1976. On the relative abundance of migrant birds from the north temperate zone in tropical habitats. Wilson Bull., 88:433-458.

Keast, A. and E. S. Morton
   1980. Migrant birds in the neotropics: ecology, behavior, distribution, and conservation. Smithsonian Inst. Press, Washington, D.C.

Kendeigh, C. S.
   1947. Bird population studies in the coniferous forest biome during a spruce budworm outbreak. Ontario Dept. Lands and Forests Bull., 1:1-100.

King, J. R.
   1974. Seasonal allocation of time and energy resources in birds. Pp. 4-70, in R.L Paynter, ed. Avian energetics. Publ. Nuttall Ornith. Club 15, Cambridge, Mass.

Knight, D. H.
   1975. A phytosociological analysis of species-rich tropical forest on Barro Colorado Island, Panama. Ecol. Monogr., 45:259-284.

Krebs, J. R.
   1973. Social learning and the significance of mixed-species flocking of Chickadees (*Parus* spp.). Can. J. Zool., 51:275-288.

Lack, D.
   1968. Bird migration and natural selection. Oikos, 19:1-9.

Lack, D. and P. Lack.
   1972. Wintering warblers of Jamaica. Living Bird, 11:129-153.

Leck, C. F.
   1972. Seasonal changes in feeding pressures of fruit- and nectar-eating birds in Panama. Condor, 74:54-60.

Leigh, E. G.
   1975. Structure and climate in tropical rain forests. Ann. Rev. Syst. and Ecol., 6:67-86.

Leigh, E. G. and N. Smythe
   1979. Leaf production, leaf consumption, and the regulation of folivory on Barro Colorado Island. Pp. 33:49, in G. Montgomery, ed. The ecology of arboreal folivores. Smithsonian Inst. Press, Washington, D.C.

MacArthur, R.
1958. Population ecology of some warblers of northeastern coniferous forests. Ecol., 39:599-619.
1972. Geographical ecology: patterns in the distribution of species. New York, Harper & Row.

Marler, P.
1957. Specific distinctiveness in the communication signals of birds. Behaviour, 11:13-39.

Mcdiarmid, R. W., R. E. Ricklefs and M. F. Foster
1977. Dispersal of *Stemmadenia donnell-smithii* (Apocynaceae) by birds. Biotropica, 9:9-25.

Mckey, D.
1975. The ecology of coevolved dispersal systems. Pp. 159-191, in L. E. Gilbert and P. H. Raven, eds. Coevolution of animals and plants. Univ. Texas Press, Austin, Texas.

Meyer de Shauensee, R.
1970. A guide to the birds of South America. Livingston Co., Pennsylvania.

Miller, A. H.
1963. Avifauna of an american equatorial cloud forest. Univ. Calif. Publ. Zool., 66:1-72.

Mook, L. J.
1963. Birds and the spruce budworm. Pp. 268-271, in R. F. Morris, ed. Dynamic of epidemic spruce budworm populations. Mem. Ent. Soc. Canada No. 3.

Morris, R. A., A. Chesire, A. Miller, and D. Mott
1958. The numerical response of avian and mammalian predators during a gradation of the spruce budworm. Ecology, 39:487-494.

Morse, D. H.
1970. Ecological aspects of some mixed species foraging flocks of birds. Ecol. Monogr., 40:119-168.

Morse, D. H.
1971. The foraging ecology of warblers isolated on small islands. Ecology, 52:216-228.

Morse, D. H.
1976. Variables affecting the density and territory size of breeding spruce-woods warblers. Ecology, 57:290-301.

Morse, D. H.
1978. Populations of Bay-breasted and Cape May Warblers during an outbreak of spruce budworms. Wilson Bull., 90:404-413.

Morse, D. H.
1979. Habitat use of the Blackpoll Warbler. Wilson Bull., 91:234-243.

Morton, E. S.
1971. Food and migration of the Eastern Kingbird in Panama. Auk, 88:925-926.

Morton, E. S.
1980. Adaptation to seasonal changes by migrant landbirds in the Panama Canal Zone. Pp. 437-457 in A. Keast and E. S. Morton, eds. Migrant birds in the neotropics: ecology, behavior, distribution, and conservation. Smithsonian Inst. Press, Washington, D.C.

Moynihan, M.
1962. The organization and probable evolution of some mixed species flocks of neotropical birds. Smithsonian Misc. Coll., 143:1-140.

Munn, C. A. and J. W. Terborgh
1979. Multispecies territoriality in neotropical foraging flocks. Condor, 81:338-347.

Myers, J. P.
   1980. Territoriality and flocking by Buff-breasted Sandpipers: variations in nonbreeding dispersion. Condor, 82:241-250.

Nisbet, I. C.T. and Lord Medway
   1972. Dispersion, population ecology, and migration of Eastern Reed Warblers (*Acrocephalus orientalis*) wintering in Malaysia. Ibis, 114:451-494.

Nolan, V.
   1979. Ecology and behavior of *Dendroica discolor*. A. O. U. Ornith. Monogr. No. 20.

Orians, G. H.
   1961. The ecology of blackbird (*Agelaius*) social systems. Ecol. Monogr., 31:285-312.

Page, G. and D. F. Whitacre
   1975. Raptor predation on wintering shorebirds. Condor, 77:73-83.

Paine, R. T.
   1971. The measurement and application of the calorie to ecological problems. Ann. Rev. Ecol. Syst., 2:145-164.

Parnell, J. F.
   1969. Habitat relations of the parulidae during spring migration. Auk, 86:505-521.

Partridge, L.
   1976. Field and laboratory observation on the foraging and feeding techniques of blue tits (*Parus caeruleus*) and Coal Tits (*P. ater*) in relation to their habitats. Anim. Behav., 24:534-544.

Payne, R. B.
   1972. Mechanisms and control of molt. Pp. 103-155, in D. S. Farner and J. R. King, eds. Avian Biology vol. 2, Academic Press, London.

Pitelka, F. A.
   1959. Numbers, breeding schedule, and territoriality in Pectoral Sandpipers in northern Alaska. Condor, 61:233-264.

Pitelka, F. A., R. T. Holmes, and S. F. Maclean
   1974. Adaptive significance of social organization in arctic sandpipers. Amer. Zool., 14:185-204.

Powell, G. V.N.
   1974. Experimental analysis of the social value of flocking by starlings. Anim. Behav., 22:501-505.
   1980. Migrant participation in neotropical mixed species bird flocks. Pp. 477-485, in A. Keast and E. S. Morton, eds. Migrant birds in the Neotropics: ecology, behavior, distribution, and conservation. Smithsonian Inst. Press, Washington, D.C.

Pulliam, H. R.
   1973. On the advantages of flocking. J. Theor. Biol., 38:419-422.

Rabenold, K. N.
   1978. Foraging strategies, diversity, and seasonality of bird communities of Appalachian spruce-fir forest. Ecol. Monogr., 48:397-424.
   1980. The Black-throated Green Warbler in Panama: geographic and seasonal comparisons of foraging. Pp. 297-309 in A. Keast and E. S. Morton, eds. Migrant birds in the Neotropics: ecology, behavior, distribution, and conservation. Smithsonian Inst. Press, Washington, D.C.

Rappole, J. H. and D. W. Warner
   1980. Ecological aspects of migrant bird behavior in Veracruz, Mexico. Pp. 353-395, in A. Keast and E. S. Morton, eds. Migrant birds in the Neotropics: ecology, behavior, distribution, and conservation. Smithsonian Inst. Press, Washington D.C.

Rappole, J. H., M. A. Ramos, R. J. Oehlenschlager, D. W. Warner, and B. P. Christopher
    1980. Timing of migration and route selection in North American songbirds. Proc. First Welder Wildlife Found. Symp., 1:199-214.

Ridgely, R. D.
    1976. A guide to the birds of Panama. Princeton Univ. Press, Princeton, N. J.

Root, R. B.
    1967. The niche exploitation pattern of the Blue-gray Gnatcatcher. Ecol. Monogr., 37:317-350.

Salomenson, F.
    1955. The evolutionary significance of bird migration. Biol. Medd. (Dan.), 22:1-62.

Schoener, T.
    1968. The *Anolis* lizards of Bimini: resource partitioning in a complex fauna. Ecology, 49:704-726.

Schwartz, P.
    1964. The Northern Waterthrush in Venezuela. Living Bird, 2:169-184.

Sealy, S. P.
    1979. Extralimital nesting of Bay-breasted Warblers: response to forest tent caterpillars? Auk, 96:600-603.

Skutch, A. F.
    1957. Migrant warblers in their Central American homes. Pp. 275-286, in L. Griscom and A. Sprunt, eds. The warblers of North America. Devin-Adair, New York.

Slud, P.
    1960. Birds of Finca "La Selva": a tropical wet forest locality. Bull. Amer. Mus. Nat. Hist., 121:49-148.
    1964. The birds of Costa Rica (distribution and ecology). Bull. Amer. Mus. Nat. Hist., 128:1-430.

Snow, B. K. and D. W. Snow
    1971. The feeding ecology of tanagers and honeycreepers in Trinidad. Auk, 88:291-322.

Snow, D. W.
    1962a. A field study of the Black-and White Manakin, *Manacus manacus*, in Trinidad. Zoologica, 47:65-107.
    1962b. A field study of the Golden-headed Manakin, *Pipra erythrocephala*, in Trinidad. Zoologica, 47:183-198.

Stiles, E. W.
    1980. Patterns of fruit presentation and seed dispersal in bird-disseminated woody plants in the eastern deciduous forest. Amer. Nat., 5:677-688.

Stiles, G.
    1980. Evolutionary implications of habitat relations between permanent and winter resident land birds in Costa Rica. Pp. 421-432 in A. Keast and E. S. Morton, eds. migrant birds in the Neotropics: ecology, behavior, distribution, and conservation. Smithsonian Inst. Press, Washington, D.C.

Terborgh, J. W. and J. W. Faaborg
    1980. Factors affecting the distribution and abundance of North American migrants in the eastern Caribbean region. Pp. 145-157 in A. Keast and E. S. Morton, eds. Migrant birds in the neotropics: ecology, behavior, distribution, and conservation. Smithsonian Inst. Press, Washington, D.C.

Tinbergen, N., M. Impekoven and D. Franck.
    1967. An experiment on spacing-out as a defense against predation. Behaviour, 28:307-321.

Tramer, E. J.
1974. Proportions of wintering North American birds in disturbed and undisturbed tropical habitats. Condor, 76:460-464.

Tramer, E. J. and T. R. Kemp
1980. Foraging ecology of migrant and resident warblers and vireos in the highlands of Costa Rica. Pp. 285-296, in A. Keast and E. S. Morton, eds. Migrant birds in the Neotropics: ecology, behavior, distribution, and conservation. Smithsonian Inst. Press, Washington, D.C.

Von Haartman, L.
1968. The evolution of resident versus migratory habit in birds: some considerations. Ornis Fennica, 45:1-7.

Wiley, R. H.
1971. Cooperative roles in mixed flocks of antwrens (Formicariidae). Auk 88:881-892.

Williamson, P.
1971. Feeding ecology of Red-eyed Vireos and associated foliage-gleaning birds. Ecol. Monogr., 41:129-152.

Willis, E. O.
1966. The role of migrant birds at swarms of army ants. Living Bird, 5:187-231.
1967. The behavior of Bicolored Antbirds. Univ. Calif. Publ. Zool., 79:1-132.
1972. The behavior of the Spotted Antbird. A. O. U. Ornith. Monogr. No. 10.
1974. Populations and local extinctions of birds on Barro Colorado Island, Panama. Ecol. Monogr., 49:153-169.
1976. Seasonal changes in the invertebrate litter fauna on Barro Colorado Island, Panama. Revt. Bras. Biol., 36:643-657.
1980. Ecological roles of migratory and resident birds on Barro Colorado Island, Panama. Pp. 205-227, in A. Keast and E. S. Morton, eds. Migrant birds in the Neotropics: ecology, behavior, distribution, and conservation. Smithsonian Inst. Press, Washington, D.C.

Willis, E. O. and E. Eisenmann
1979. An annotated checklist of the birds of Barro Colorado Island. Smithsonian Contributions in Zool. No. 292.

Wolda, H.
1978. Fluctuations in abundance of tropical insects. Amer. Nat., 112:1017-1045.

WITHDRAWN